The Amish Cook at Home

The Amish Cook at Home

Simple Pleasures of Food, Family, and Faith

LOVINA EICHER with KEVIN WILLIAMS

PHOTOGRAPHY by BETSY BLANTON

Andrews McMeel
Publishing, LLC
Kansas City

08 09 10 11 12 POA 10 9 8 7 6 5 4 3 2 1

Library of Congress Cataloging-in-Publication Data
Eicher, Lovina.
   The Amish cook at home: simple pleasures of food, family,
and faith/Lovina Eicher and Kevin Williams.
         p. cm.
   Includes index.
   ISBN-13: 978-0-7407-7372-3
   ISBN-10: 0-7407-7372-0
 1. Amish Cookery. 2. Amish—Social life and customs.
I. Williams, Kevin. II. Title.
   TX715.E3274 2008
   641.5'66—dc22

                                        2008006991

Photos pages 61, 104, 144 © istockphoto.com

www.andrewsmcmeel.com
www.amishcookonline.com

ATTENTION: SCHOOLS AND BUSINESSES
Andrews McMeel books are available at quantity discounts
with bulk purchase for educational, business, or sales
promotional use. For information, please write to:
Special Sales Department, Andrews McMeel Publishing, LLC,
1130 Walnut Street, Kansas City, Missouri 64106.

In loving memory of Elizabeth Coblentz
(1936–2002)

contents

ACKNOWLEDGMENTS
ix

INTRODUCTION
xi

INDEX
202

⊰ Acknowledgments ⊱

From Lovina: Special thanks to my husband, Joe, and my children, Elizabeth, Susan, Verena, Benjamin, Loretta, Joseph, Lovina, and Kevin, for their patience and support while I took time out of our busy lives to do this book.

Thanks also to my sisters, Susan, Verena, and Emma, and brother-in-law, Jacob, for their encouragement. And special thanks to my editor, Kevin Williams, for his patience and support. May God bless all of you.

From Kevin: Acknowledgments on a project like this are similar to assembling an Amish casserole: You throw everything in a pot and hope you aren't missing something. So, here's my attempt at acknowledgments, and if I've missed something or someone, I apologize.

This book would not have been possible without the dedication and hard work of the Amish Cook herself, Lovina Eicher. She was wonderful to work with and always willing to set aside time to work on the book, no easy task with eight children living under her roof.

A thank-you to my far better half, Rachel, who was a constant source of support, encouragement, patience, and impromptu editing. Thanks also to my parents, Jim and Rita, and brother, Geoff, for their patience as this project was shepherded to completion.

The entire team at Andrews McMeel, many of whom I probably never had the pleasure of working with directly, deserves a hearty helping of appreciation for producing this book and making it look "bookstore ready." I'd specifically like to thank Andrews McMeel publisher Kirsty Melville for bringing the project to fruition, and Jean Lucas, Lane Butler, and Julie Stillman for their wonderfully patient, precise, and accommodating editing.

A special thank-you also to Betsy Blanton and her assistant, Nick Dellaposta, for their artful and respectful photography. They truly captured the essence of Amish life without violating it.

Last, but not least, I need to extend a full-course Amish feastful of gratitude to my literary agent, Janis Donnaud. Janis was the equivalent of the cavalry coming. She really was the right ingredient at the right time for *The Amish Cook at Home*.

Introduction

by Kevin Williams

A CALENDAR FULL OF FOOD

Colorful corn casserole. A loaf of still-warm sourdough bread. A plate of juicy sliced tomatoes. Meaty chicken breasts fresh from the grill. A kettle of chunked beef swimming in a rich broth. A pot of homemade tomato soup. Sliced fresh-from-the-garden carrots. And zucchini. Lots of zucchini. Zucchini bread. Zucchini casserole. Zucchini jam. And something sweet to top it off: homemade cookies, perhaps? A generously iced cake? This may sound like a feast meant for a New England church potluck supper or a family picnic. But it's not. This is supper in an Amish home, where there is a daily smorgasbord of delicious dinners. The vegetable dishes are fresh from the garden. The meats were raised and fed on the premises. The chickens roam freely on the farmstead.

The family supper is a ritual that has been under assault in most of America, challenged by soccer games, Nintendo, and working teenagers. But among the Amish supper remains sacred: a time to be together, to reflect, to enjoy one another's company.

MEET LOVINA EICHER

Supper comes at the end of a long day. There's much work to do before everyone sits down together: Twenty quarts of beets need canning. A mountain of laundry awaits. A daughter has a skinned knee, a son has the sniffles. A fight over a toy needs settling. Thirteen-year-old Elizabeth needs help with her homework. A supper needs to be cooked. And bread baked. Buttons sewn. Tomatoes picked. Dishes washed. Some bills to pay. Prayers to recite. Weeds to pull. Another skinned knee to doctor. Welcome to the world of Lovina Eicher. And she's unfazed by the eight growing children building their lives around her. "I wouldn't want it any other way," Lovina once told me as I marveled at her calm composure despite a daily grind that might make the average suburban housewife head for the exits. Not Lovina. It's a calm cultivated by generations of homemaker housewives before her, an ingenuity, stoicism, and sense of purpose inherited from the Amish who came to the Americas to escape persecution in Europe two centuries ago.

A round face, a ready smile, and the ability to "multitask" long before it became trendy in cubicles and cars across America define Lovina's life. It is this calm sense of simplicity, this living connection to a time when life wasn't so fast-paced, that has endeared Lovina to millions of readers of "The Amish Cook" newspaper column.

The column is not something Lovina had expected to be juggling along with her many other daily duties. Running a household

Popular 'Amish Cook' columnist dies suddenly during visit here

'Amish Cook' was in town to sign books
By DARLA McFARLAND *The Examiner* (Independence, Missouri)

Elizabeth Coblentz, author of the syndicated cooking column "The Amish Cook," died Tuesday night at St. Mary's Hospital of Blue Springs after collapsing in her room at a Blue Springs hotel.

Coblentz, 66, is believed to have suffered an aortic aneurysm. An autopsy is expected to determine the exact cause of death.

The author was visiting the area to attend a book signing, sponsored by *The Examiner*, at Independence Center today. She wrote her first column in 1991 and began running in *The Examiner Extra* each Wednesday in 1999. The column in today's *Examiner Extra* edition, which was printed on Tuesday, is her last new article.

Coblentz wrote her column by hand from her farm near Geneva in northern Indiana. Her writing shared not only cooking tips and recipes but news and observations of her rural life. She was part of the Old Order Amish, who live without electricity, plumbing and automobiles. She leaves behind eight children and many grandchildren. Her husband, Ben Coblentz, died a few years ago.

Coblentz was traveling with her editor, Kevin Williams, and two of her daughters, Verena and Susan. The four drove down from Indiana on a brief tour.

Tuesday in Quincy, Ill., 300 to 400 people showed up to meet Coblentz, said Mike Hilfrink, executive editor of the *Quincy Herald-Whig*, the first newspaper to publish her column.

Coblentz' next stop was to be Ottawa, Kan.

Williams, speaking with *The Examiner* late Tuesday, said Coblentz had collapsed earlier in the evening but revived quickly. She refused to go to the hospital. She collapsed again about 8 p.m. and never regained consciousness. Doctors pronounced her dead about 9:30 p.m.

Williams said Coblentz' daughters were anxious to return to their family in Indiana.

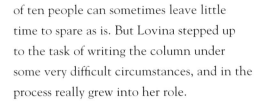

of ten people can sometimes leave little time to spare as is. But Lovina stepped up to the task of writing the column under some very difficult circumstances, and in the process really grew into her role.

THE BEGINNING

I was a young journalism student when I first met Lovina's mother, Elizabeth Coblentz. An eighteen-year-old soon-to-be-sophomore in college, I hoped to one day be an editor or newspaper owner. But this chance encounter at the rural Coblentz farmstead in Indiana would take my life in a drastically different direction.

I was on assignment for a tiny magazine (a college student will take whatever work necessary to fatten up that all-important portfolio), and I was assigned to write a story about the Amish. A city boy with no experience with the Amish, I quickly found myself captivated and enchanted by their profoundly different existence. I thought others might want a peek into this very different lifestyle, so drawing upon my journalism studies I—on a lark—asked Elizabeth if she might like to try writing a weekly newspaper column that I would attempt to syndicate. Never mind that I had no clue what I was doing. But the odd coupling worked, and soon the column was finding an audience in small and medium-sized Midwestern newspapers. Elizabeth and I enjoyed an eleven-year run as journalism's most unconventional pair. She'd share what happened in her life each week, along with a recipe, and I'd get it out to the newspapers. And then it all tragically came crashing down.

THE AMISH COOK

The drive back home was exhausting. I hadn't slept but a fitful few hours the night before, and I was overcome with a mixture of shock, guilt, and grief. It all seemed so surreal: the paramedics, the hospital vigil, the good-bye. And now we were heading back home, one less person in the car. An empty space.

Missouri's miles crept by on the endless drive back to Indiana. This trip had started as a celebration of sorts. Elizabeth, accompanied by two of her six daughters—Verena and Susan—and I were making a rare trip to meet fans of the column to commemorate over ten years of writing. Our first stop had been a success by any standard. Approximately four hundred people had awaited Elizabeth in Quincy, Illinois. Elizabeth signed copies of cookbooks and smiled politely as well-wishers came through to meet her. *The Quincy Herald-Whig* had been the first newspaper to take a chance on "The Amish Cook" column back in 1991, so this was our opportunity to show some appreciation.

As Missouri moved like misery outside the car windows, Susan decided to add a pinch of normalcy to the ingredients of our day. During the happier journey westward not twenty-four hours earlier, she had begun compiling a list of license plates, trying to find one from each state, methodically recording new sightings in a notebook. This kept us all focused and busy on the way back. The return trip was punctuated by occasional shouts of "There's Maine!" "I think I saw Idaho!" and "Wisconsin!" That game was a welcome respite

from our grief—the Amish appreciate such simple pleasures, an endearing trait I admire. We would finally arrive at the Coblentz farmstead around 11 P.M., where I fell into a bear hug by Jacob Schwartz, Elizabeth's son-in-law. But, for me, the journey was not over. After we gathered and grieved in the dark driveway, far from city lights, I announced: "I need to go," I turned to the small crowd in the driveway. "I really need to go."

"Oh, no, stay. We've got an extra bed, you can get started early in the morning," one of Elizabeth's daughters offered.

"I can't, I just really have to go," I said, without elaborating.

My mind drifted to almost ten years earlier when "The Amish Cook" column got one of its first big breaks. A well-known food columnist had committed suicide. I started getting calls the next morning.

"The Lazy Gourmet killed himself last night," the editor of *The Bryan Times* in Ohio told me matter-of-factly.

"Oh, that's terrible, I'm so sorry," I said.

"Yeah. It happens. So, we now have space to add 'The Amish Cook.' How much per week?" The editor asked.

I would get several calls like that over the week ahead, doubling the column's readership in a matter of days. This was 1992, and space was scarce at newspapers. Ten years later, in 2002, in the age of shrinking newspapers and the ubiquitous Internet, it was even more scarce. I knew that syndicates—my competition—would be hungrily coveting the valuable empty space left in the paper once word of Elizabeth's death spread. Although the scope, speed, and size of the spread would surprise even me.

It was 11 P.M. when I left the Coblentz farmstead. I had only hours before editors would walk into their newsrooms and read the AP wire. I said my good-byes and drove home rapidly through the Indiana darkness. Surreptitiously, Elizabeth and I—only weeks

Activity shifts from indoor to outdoor after a long winter spent in front of the coal-stove, playing board games, reading, and catching up on sewing. Meals on the front porch, the first seeds in the garden, and the colorful blooms of flowers add a buzz of outdoor activity to the Eicher farmstead.

earlier—had discussed the possibility that one day she wouldn't be around to write the column. What should we do? She said that she would like to see one of her daughters "pick up the pen" and continue. Not thinking the end was so near, Elizabeth and I never got far enough in our talk for her to indicate to me *which* daughter should take over. We would have to sort that out later. For the moment, I just wanted to fulfill my end of the bargain to allow the column to be passed to another generation. I sat at my computer and sent out a middle-of-the-night message to all "The Amish Cook" newspapers: "The column will continue." I clicked the "send" button. It was just after 1 A.M.

And sure enough, the next morning the news of Elizabeth's death did hit the newswires. The following days were a whirlwind of interviews with CNN, the *Los Angeles Times*, the *Wall Street Journal*, the *New York Times*, and the *San Francisco Chronicle*. The column had resonated. I had always thought that it had, but now I knew the extent.

Elizabeth Coblentz was a feisty, sometimes ornery, woman. While many Amish women hew to the stereotype of quiet and semi-submissive, Elizabeth had a fiery maverick streak that complemented my more subdued manner. We were a journalistic odd couple who somehow found a way to bridge our generational and cultural canyon with a column.

Steely with a buggy-whip and domestic with a pie, Elizabeth was a living dichotomy. It was her complexity, her sense of self, that made her the Amish Cook. Some Amish in her area weren't overly fond of her column writing, deeming it too worldly or showy. "Jealousy!" Elizabeth would simply scoff.

But Elizabeth also had a sweet streak. After I had a particularly painful breakup with a girlfriend she sent me a two-page letter written in longhand. "Kevin, never look back, only forward," she wrote. "This was for the best." And it was.

One of my most cherished memories of her was a time when we were working on our first book together, *The Amish Cook*. After sitting around for days while the photographer chronicled Elizabeth's life in pictures, I was feeling lazy. "Elizabeth, there has to be *something* I can do for you. I feel like a freeloader." But Elizabeth wouldn't have any of it. I did hear her mention earlier in my visit about her garden being full of unwanted thistles. So I went out to the garden to clear it. I gradually became aware of a few odd stares from passing buggies. But soon Elizabeth joined me. I pulled thistles and she grabbed a hoe and gently kneaded the soil like soft dough. She quietly sang as I thrust thistle weeds over a fence into the pasture. We worked together for a while, the sun beating down on our backs. I'm not sure if we spoke a word to each other that afternoon, but we didn't have to.

One time, shortly before our ill-fated trip to Missouri, Elizabeth and I were driving on an errand into town. As my speedometer clocked 60 in a 45 mph zone, I found myself with the all-too-familiar scene of police lights whirling in the rearview mirror. I pulled over and rolled down my window. I respectfully told Elizabeth to let me doing the talking, I'd get us out of this.

"Son, have you been drinking?" the officer asked cautiously.

"Only some pop!" Elizabeth quickly quipped. The sight of the grandmotherly, black-bonnet-clad Amish woman in the passenger seat next to me probably surprised him.

The officer chuckled and walked away. The abrupt honesty and innocence endeared her to the officer much as it did her readers. Elizabeth helped me, and I like to think I gave her something in return. I think of her often and I miss her, sometimes more with the passage of time as I come to appreciate the fragility of life. I came to her in the twilight of her life, but I was still in the morning of mine, and she taught me about tomorrow.

FINDING THE NEW AMISH COOK

The Coblentz daughters just sort of naturally gravitated toward Lovina as the new Amish Cook. I would have been happy with any of them. The Coblentz daughters are in many ways like the sisters I never had. There was never one "aha" moment when it was decided that Lovina would take over; we all just agreed that she'd be a great one for the role. And so she picked up the pen. Her first words, appearing in October 2002, just weeks after Elizabeth's death, were:

I am nervous and not sure how to begin this . . . .
It is very difficult for me to take over this column.
I will never be able to write like my dear mother,
but I will try my best.

I warned Lovina when she took over the column that readers would give her a chance for a while based solely on their affection for her mother. But over time, I told her, you have to earn the audience yourself. And Lovina has. The column has grown in the years since her mother passed away. I think people connect with Lovina's genuine goodness, which shows through in the column.

Good is a very bland word, tossed around in conversation almost as an afterthought. That pie was *good*. The movie was *good*. What a *good* book. *Good* is almost rendered meaningless, a flavorless filler when one can't find a better adjective. It's a shame that such a word has been stripped of its original meaning: one letter away from God.

To me, the Eichers have come to personify a goodness missing in much of the world. I've watched Lovina and her husband, Joe, seemingly effortlessly move from sitting on her mother's front porch swing as a courting couple to getting married, now with a home and a family of their own. During this time, I've sometimes

seemed stuck, trying to find my bearings in an increasingly complicated world: one foot firmly in the simplicity of Amish existence, the other in the fast-paced current of the twenty-first century, swirling toward an unknown tomorrow. If I can find my footing and one day have a family and life half as kind and pure as the Eichers, I will have found happiness.

There is a tendency to over-romanticize the Amish in American pop culture. There are bad apples among the Amish just as there are in any other group. The Amish are divided by jealousies, rivalries, and pettiness. Even with this knowledge, though, I still find myself fascinated by the culture and religion. I think it's because there are Amish families like the Eichers that provide us all with a living link to a time when family, faith, and food were the cornerstones of our daily life. There is, at its core, a resiliency, an admirable stubbornness to the Amish. While most of us embrace technology with little thought to its eventual impact, the Amish take the long view. Change isn't a given, it's a choice. The Amish have found a way to exert control over a process that usually works the other way.

THE NEW GENERATION

In many ways Lovina and I have a closer relationship than her mother and I had, but I think that's natural. Lovina and her husband are my age, sharing my same generational experiences and events even though we have two very different ways of life. I live in a world of BlackBerry PDAs, iPods, text messaging, and e-mail. Lovina lives in a world of blackberries and raspberries, home canning, quilting, child rearing, and the slow cadence of a buggy ride. But despite our differences, we make the column work. Lovina, using the age-old craft of handwritten letters, pens her column, sticks it in an envelope, stamps it, and puts it in the hands of the mailman. Days later, it appears in my mailbox, at which point I use all the twenty-first-century tools at my disposal to get the column out to millions of readers each week. This cookbook has taken shape the same way: lots of mail and lots of talk—over-the-back-fence-type talk. This cookbook couldn't bend to the fast pace of our e-mail-driven world. Like a slow Sunday pot roast, it had to simmer. This cookbook is the culmination of many months of conversation, writing, and Amish wisdom.

Sometimes, it was difficult to meld our two very different ways to create this book. At one point toward the end, when I was pressing Lovina for some more exact recipe measurements, she exclaimed, slightly exasperated: "Don't the editors understand that the Amish cook by just guessing how much goes in?" Most of the time Amish cooks guess right, based on experience forged through generations of knowledge. We tried to put these "guesses" into exact measurements and pass them on to you.

Lovina's Michigan home is a passel of lively, happy children chasing fireflies, making snow angels, reading books, learning to bake, learning to do chores, playing outdoors. If I close my eyes, I can sometimes see Elizabeth sitting on a rocking chair on Lovina's front porch, nodding with pleasure. I'm still learning, this time from Lovina, about the simple joys of life. I hope this cultural cookbook allows others to learn also. Pull up a chair and enjoy a journey through the seasonal rhythms of Amish life in the pages ahead.

Our world, with its indoor malls, flip-of-the-switch heated homes, and ice-cold air-conditioning no longer is tethered to the whims of nature as it once was. Feel like a swim in January? There's probably a heated indoor pool somewhere nearby. Want ripe tomatoes in February? Just go to the nearest supermarket. Ice cream, once a treat of winter, is now a summer staple.

Day-to-day Amish life revolves around seasonal rhythms. There's a reawakening of sorts each spring, when Amish families emerge from their winter coal-fired cocoons and taste the first fresh bounty of April's warmth. Summer is a time of fishing holes, pleasant buggy rides, and barefoot work and play. Autumn brings with it the awareness that another cold winter is approaching and life takes on a more rapid pace as the garden is finished, firewood is stored, and canning is completed. Winter is a time of cozy coal fires, puzzles and games in the evening, and snowball fights and sleigh rides. This book is organized around the seasons in an attempt to capture the same rhythm that most Amish live their lives by. Most of this book is in Lovina's voice, which has a unique authenticity. Context and depth is added with some sidebars and stories by other Eicher family members and by me.

Perhaps the Amish most experience the seasons through food. Spring, summer, and fall are a time to enjoy the fresh vegetables coming from the garden. Almost every Amish homemaker has one. It's central to the self-sufficiency that the Amish still strive to achieve. So the "warm season" chapters are filled with vegetable recipes. We could have devoted the entire summer just to zucchini, the Amish homemaker's favorite versatile vegetable! Fall and winter are the time to tackle the messier job of butchering meat.

Most Amish keep some livestock to provide fresh meat and milk for their family. While they enjoy meat through freezing and canning year-round, we've put most of the meat recipes in these chapters. But we hope readers enjoy the culinary creations through all months of the year!

Like many traditions in Amish culture, culinary rules are slowly changing. Fifty years ago it would have been very uncommon for an Amish person to venture into any sort of supermarket unless it was to purchase something in bulk. But for a variety of complex reasons, the traditionally agrarian Amish culture is evolving into something different. More and more Amish men are working in factories or in service-type jobs. As fewer Amish farm, pure self-sufficiency breaks down, the "outside world" intrudes more and more, and their food reflects this. As the Amish morph away from a purely agrarian society to a less isolated one, they are venturing into grocery stores more. Amish cooks love to experiment and try different foods, so some of the store-bought ingredients included in this book's recipes are not anomalies; they are an accurate reflection of a changing Amish culinary culture.

This book will hopefully serve as a road map of sorts through the seasons of Amish cooking. The recipes and the order were carefully selected to reflect not only what the Eichers and other Amish might be eating for a meal, but also *when*. Use this book as a culinary calendar for Amish cooking. When autumn arrives and you're in the mood for a dish using apples, this book will provide some ideas and inspiration. In addition to the food, we've tried to add some educational "side streets" that allow the reader to experience the whole year as an Old Order Amish person would, including glimpses into events like weddings, funerals, tax time, and holidays. So go forward and enjoy the journey. We think you'll find lots of tasty stops along the way.

THE EICHER FAMILY

Mother and Amish Cook Columnist: **Lovina**

Father and Husband: **Joe**

The Children and Their Birthdays:

Elizabeth	June 14, 1994
Susan	January 24, 1996
Verena	December 10, 1997
Benjamin	July 14, 1999
Loretta	July 1, 2000
Joseph	July 24, 2002
Lovina	May 18, 2004
Kevin	September 2, 2005

spring

Beseech Thee, beloved and merciful Father, that Thou wouldst let Thy Word, which we have heard and received, be powerful and genuine in the heart of each one of us, and be fruitful, bearing fruit that remains until eternal life. May we through it be not only born again, but completely turned about, changed, and renewed.

—Excerpt from Amish prayer after
the sermon, English translation

Spring is about everything being new again.

I love seeing the grass turn greener and the rhubarb stalks sprouting, and witnessing the new stuff all growing—there is nothing better than fresh homegrown food.

By the time March rolls around, I am tired of winter and am ready for spring, my favorite season of the year. Spring always makes me think of new foals running out in the fields with their mothers, fresh flowers, and sunlight later in the day. Spring is also usually when we get baby chicks that are ready to be cared for and raised.

Another highlight of spring—at least when I was a child—was the arrival of my birthday each year on May 22. As an adult, I don't look forward to it quite so much! I also enjoyed helping my mom plant the garden, a tradition I now share with my own daughters, who seem to enjoy this time as much as I did.

Spring brings with it an excitement among our children; they know that school will soon be closing for the term. Personally, I love to see the tulips and Easter lilies pop up, and I get pleasure from planting flowers and hanging pots and then watching the finches build nests in them on our front porch. Meanwhile, even my husband, Joe, is always excited about what spring brings—especially the chance to go look for mushrooms in the nearby woods.

A WILD WELCOME

Nature provides the first taste of spring with perennial plants that grow "wild" around here: rhubarb, dandelions, asparagus, and onions, to name a few favorites. Rhubarb begins spreading its big leaves, ready to be used in shortcakes, pies, jams, and other family favorites. Wild asparagus begins peeping through in patches, and green onions, with their flavorful taste, are a sure sign of spring. Bright red strawberries, which thrive in the coolness of spring, also begin blooming. But perhaps the most exciting signal is when our favorite foods finally find their way onto our supper plates. Perhaps the most eagerly awaited is the arrival of young, tender dandelions.

DANDELIONS

Dandelion greens are a hit in this household, at least with some of us. Getting ten people to all agree on a single food is a near impossibility. But for those of us who agree about dandelion greens, dandelion salads are enjoyed for the brief spell that they're in season. If we're lucky, we'll have three to four weeks in late April and early May of ideal dandelion-harvesting conditions. The green leaves need to be picked and eaten while they are young, otherwise the taste becomes bitter quickly.

For collecting the dandelion greens, I usually just use a stainless-steel bowl. If it is windy, I use an ice cream bucket or some other deeper dish so they won't blow away. We end up also collecting grass and leaves in with them, so we always bring the greens inside and wash them three or four times until the water is clear.

Out of all our children, Susan seems to like dandelion greens the most. My daughter Elizabeth won't even eat them; she says they "taste like grass." I asked her if she had ever tasted grass and she said "no." Daughter Verena has tried dandelions a couple of times but just can't seem to "get" the taste. Joe, Susan, and I are the only ones who will really eat them now. I think the children will all come to enjoy them over time. I remember when I was a girl I didn't like dandelions either, but I began to like them as I got older. Now I really enjoy them.

I fix my dandelion green salad using a mixture of dressing and vinegar to make it smooth, and then I add salt and milk and it becomes a homemade sour cream of sorts, which I pour over the greens. I also dice hard-boiled eggs to mix in, which gives it all a better taste. And then, to top it all off, I steam some potatoes and put the whole dandelion green salad over them.

There are so many recipes that can be prepared from dandelions. Some use them in soups, homemade wines, jellies, and salads. Here are a couple of our family's favorites.

DANDELION SOUR CREAM SALAD

Serves 4 to 6

This is a recipe for dandelions smothered in our favorite homemade sour cream. You can, however, use just the sour cream part for other seasonal greens as well. This same sour cream is great when used with in-season, fresh-from-the-garden lettuce and endive. Home-cured ham also goes well with it. Any unused sour cream can be refrigerated for up to 2 days.

½ cup mayonnaise

1 cup apple cider vinegar

2½ cups whole milk

Salt

4 hard-boiled eggs (see page 33), diced

4 cups packed young dandelion greens

Combine the mayonnaise, vinegar, milk, and salt to taste in a quart jar. Shake until smooth. Put the eggs and dandelion greens in a large bowl and pour the sour cream mixture over them.

DANDELION JELLY

Makes 6 half-pint jars

A lot of families make homemade dandelion jelly around here. The jelly has a clearish color and a special sweetness to it. My editor has tried a peanut butter and dandelion jelly sandwich and says it is really good, but I'm not fond of peanut butter with any kind of jelly so I'll just take his word on that!

4 cups dandelion blossoms
4 cups water
1 (1½-ounce) package fruit pectin
1 teaspoon lemon extract
4½ cups sugar

In the early morning, pick the blossoms without the stems attached. Bring the water to a boil in a medium saucepan, add the blossoms, and cook for 3 minutes. Strain 3 cups of the liquid through a sieve into a bowl. Discard the blossoms. Stir the fruit pectin, lemon extract, and sugar into the liquid. Return to the saucepan, bring to a boil, and cook for 3 minutes. Immediately pour into sterilized half-pint jars and attach the seals and lids. The heat will seal the jars.

Note: See page 81 for more information on home canning.

Spring is also a special time for our children.
Warmer weather brings with it outdoor games, the end
of school, and an end to long evenings indoors.

DANDELIONS WITH GRAVY

Serves 4 to 6

This is another popular way to prepare dandelions among Amish cooks in our community. The gravy is also good over boiled or mashed potatoes, and some even eat it with pork chops or other meat.

3 to 4 strips bacon

2 tablespoons all-purpose flour

2 tablespoons water

1 cup milk

Salt and ground pepper

1 onion, chopped

1 tablespoon sugar

1 tablespoon apple cider vinegar

2 hard-boiled eggs (see page 33), chopped

4 cups packed young dandelion greens

Fry the bacon in a heavy skillet until crisp. Transfer the bacon to paper towels to drain. Stir the flour into the bacon fat and then add the water. Stir until smooth. Add the milk, and salt and pepper to taste. Continue to stir until smooth. Add the onion, sugar, and the vinegar to your taste of sweet and sour. Stir in the eggs. Pour the gravy over the dandelions and toss. Serve right away.

WHY I LIKE SPRING
by Elizabeth Eicher, age thirteen

Spring is my favorite season. I love to watch the frisky foals running alongside the mares in the green pastures.

I also like to watch the first robins scratch in the dirt and peck the worms. The little baby robins stretch their necks asking for food, and then I see the mother robins feed the worms to them. On the first days of spring, I love to open the windows that have been closed all winter and then smell the fresh air of spring with the smell of the lilacs coming through from our bushes. I long for the moment when Mom says: "Today is the day that it is warm enough to go barefooted." I slip out of my shoes and socks and go run outside where the soft green grass feels warm beneath my feet. I look up at the trees and see the tiny leaves sprouting. Then I see a robin building a nest getting ready for the little ones. I hitch our pony, Stormy, to the wagon and take my brothers and sisters for a ride. I stop the pony short as I let a mother duck and her ducklings cross the road. I look up at the skies and I see no more snow clouds. I tell my brothers and sisters that I think spring is finally here!

This is a favorite recipe that I enjoy fixing for my brothers and sisters. We usually have it for breakfast, but sometimes for a change of pace we'll eat "breakfast for supper."

BREAKFAST BURRITOS
Serves 10

I like to make this breakfast for my brothers and sisters on the first warm spring mornings when we can eat outside on our porch. You can use either sausage or bacon with this recipe, but we usually use bacon. The burritos can be put into freezer bags and frozen.

2 pounds bacon	1 teaspoon salt
½ cup diced green bell pepper	1 teaspoon pepper
½ cup chopped mushrooms	10 slices Cheddar cheese
¼ cup chopped onion	10 (8½-inch) flour tortillas
½ cup margarine or butter	
15 large eggs, lightly beaten	

Preheat the oven to 350°F. Fry the bacon until crisp in a large, heavy skillet. Transfer the bacon to paper towels to drain and cool slightly, then crumble and set aside. Pour all but 2 teaspoons of the bacon grease out of the skillet, then add the bell pepper, mushrooms, and onion and fry until tender. Drain, then stir in the crumbled bacon.

In a large skillet over low heat, melt the margarine and scramble the eggs. Lay each tortilla in the center of a square of aluminum foil. Place a slice of cheese in the center of each tortilla, then divide the meat mixture equally among the tortillas, followed by the scrambled eggs. Fold the bottom of each tortilla over the filling, then fold in the sides and finish rolling up the tortilla. Wrap the burritos in the foil, then place them on a baking sheet and bake until heated through, 10 to 15 minutes. Serve with sour cream and salsa.

Kevin's note: It might be surprising to some to find a recipe for burritos in an Amish cookbook. The trend toward south-of-the-border food has been accelerating among the Amish. To find out why, see page 92.

MUSHROOMS

The warm spring rains are ideal for carpeting the forest floor with wild mushrooms; many are too dangerous to eat, but some are delicious. You have to be careful.

Mushrooms are another delicacy of spring and, like the wild dandelions, these aren't around for very long. You really have to know what you are doing to pick them. My husband, Joe, usually picks spikes, sponges, and morels.

While dandelions are in plentiful supply most years, mushrooms are more difficult to predict. Some years the conditions are better than others for mushroom hunting. Sometimes, Joe might go out every Sunday for weeks and have no luck even if he is out there all day. And then other times, he may come back with dozens. I wouldn't know which mushrooms are poisonous and which ones aren't, but Joe picked them as a boy and was taught by his father which ones are okay to eat. I'd like to go along sometime to learn. Our problem is that we don't have the woods here like we did back in Indiana. And some people don't want others hunting mushrooms in their woods.

To prepare the mushrooms we soak them in saltwater overnight, because Joe says that the saltwater cleans them. Then most of the time I either deep-fry the mushrooms or Joe grills them. The children really like them served both ways, but I think they prefer them when they are deep-fried and they can just eat them by themselves. They don't care for mushrooms when I put them on top of pizza or when I put them in burritos or something. I never could think why they don't like them on a pizza. Joe says there is nothing better than the fresh ones you find, and I agree. Store-bought mushrooms just don't taste the same.

LEARNING TO HUNT MUSHROOMS
by Joe Eicher

Dad took me along as a child to hunt mushrooms. He showed me which ones are okay and which ones aren't. We always went mushroom hunting after a thunderstorm in warming spring weather. Those seemed to be the best conditions for finding some good ones. Dad taught me that flat mushrooms that grow on or around trees are the poisonous ones. The main ones we hunted for when I was a boy were the spikes and the yellow sponges that grow around stumps. We didn't take any tools with us to gather them, just a bag to put them in.

One thing I'll never forget was when we were hunting for mushrooms once and a blue racer snake tried to attack us, but my dad was able to take care of it for us. We never did pick the morels much, since they grew up north more. Spikes and yellow sponges were our main target. The best way I like to eat them is battered and deep-fried or grilled on a pan brushed with butter.

STUFFED MUSHROOMS

Serves 4 to 6

Some years Joe doesn't have much luck finding mushrooms; it just depends on the conditions. So, even though they don't taste as good, I will buy them in the store if we don't have freshly picked ones to prepare. One simple way we like to eat fresh mushrooms is to wrap a piece of bacon around each one, put a toothpick in to hold the bacon on, and then place on a skewer and grill it. They are good like that, but stuffed mushrooms are another favorite way to eat them around here.

¼ pound bulk sausage

¼ cup diced green onion, including green parts

¾ cup mayonnaise

12 large white mushrooms, stems separated and finely chopped

½ cup shredded Cheddar cheese

Preheat the oven to 350°F. Combine the sausage and the green onion in a large skillet and brown over medium heat. Remove from the heat and stir in the mayonnaise and chopped mushroom stems. Spoon the sausage mixture into the mushroom caps. Sprinkle the cheese over the mushrooms. Place the mushrooms on a baking sheet and bake until they are heated through and the cheese is melted, about 20 minutes.

DEEP-FRIED MORELS

Serves 6 to 8

This is probably the favorite mushroom dish in our household. I know some people like to dip them in ranch dressing, but we just like to eat them plain.

¾ cup all-purpose flour

½ cup milk

1 egg, beaten

½ teaspoon salt

Olive oil for panfrying

12 to 15 large morel mushrooms

Stir the flour, milk, egg, and salt together in a large bowl. Heat 1 inch of oil in a large skillet until sizzling. Dip the mushrooms in the batter and put them in the skillet. Fry each side until golden brown. Using a slotted spoon, transfer to paper towels to drain.

ASPARAGUS

Another sure sign of spring is the green spears of asparagus poking through the thawing ground.

Just like rhubarb, asparagus will come up year after year in the same patch, so its arrival is always a signal that winter is through. Once you get an asparagus patch started it is pretty hard to get rid of. A lot of people mow theirs down in the fall, but I leave ours alone. I think it makes for stronger roots that will grow better in the spring. Most of our children like fresh asparagus when it is part of a casserole, for instance. If I just cook it and put cream over it, some of the children don't care for it. But we usually make them taste something that they may not want to try, because sometimes they are surprised and really enjoy a new food. When I was a child there were things I didn't eat that I do now.

I see a lot more asparagus grown here in Michigan. Mom never grew asparagus down in Indiana. She had everything else, but I don't know why she didn't grow asparagus. A lot of people stop and pick it where it grows wild along the roads around here.

Our family has several favorite ways to enjoy fresh asparagus.

ASPARAGUS WITH BACON-CHEESE SAUCE
Serves 4 to 6

This recipe is where I got the idea to add bacon to the asparagus-potato soup on the next page. This is a favorite dish on our spring supper table.

2 tablespoons butter

2 tablespoons all-purpose flour

1 cup milk

¼ teaspoon salt

1 cup shredded American or mild Cheddar cheese

1½ pounds asparagus, trimmed

4 to 6 slices bacon, cooked crisp and drained

Melt the butter in a medium saucepan over medium heat. Stir in the flour and cook until smooth and bubbly, about 3 minutes. Gradually whisk in the milk. Cook, whisking constantly, until the sauce has thickened. Stir in the salt and cheese until the cheese is melted. Set aside and keep warm.

Meanwhile, cook the asparagus in 1 inch of salted boiling water in a large skillet until crisp-tender, 3 to 5 minutes. Immediately drain and rinse under cold water.

Pour the sauce over the drained hot asparagus. Sprinkle with the crumbled bacon. Serve right away.

ASPARAGUS-POTATO SOUP

Serves 4 to 6

This is a thick soup. The color is light, like a cream sauce. I usually like to serve a fresh garden salad with it.

1¾ cups chicken broth

3 potatoes, peeled and cubed

⅓ cup chopped onion

1 teaspoon salt

½ pound asparagus, trimmed and cut into ½-inch pieces

1½ cups milk

2 tablespoons all-purpose flour

1 cup Velveeta or Colby cheese (cubed or sliced)

Combine the broth, potatoes, onion, and salt in a large saucepan. Cook over medium heat until the vegetables are tender, about 20 minutes. Add the asparagus and cook for 10 minutes more.

Whisk the milk and flour together well in a small bowl and whisk into the broth mixture. Stir in the cheese until melted. Pour into warmed soup bowls and serve immediately.

Variation: I once fried bacon strips and then crumbled them in with everything. It was very good! You could also sprinkle crumbled bacon over the top as a garnish.

The Amish have traditionally been absent from the aisles of supermarkets, preferring instead to let the earth yield its natural bounty after long hours of planting seeds and working the soil.

RHUBARB

A sure signal that spring has come to the Amish kitchen is the tart, tangy smell of rhubarb. It seems like it's one of those foods that people either really like the taste of or they just don't get it. Rhubarb is popular because it's easy to grow and there are just so many ways you can use it: shortcakes, spreads, cobblers, crunches, pies, jams, and even soups. One of the ways our family likes to enjoy rhubarb is in a juice!

RHUBARB JUICE

Makes 8 quarts

This recipe makes a concentrate and then you can add other juices (for instance, pineapple, or orange juice) or 7Up to it. The first year I made it, I used my sister Emma's rhubarb. I wanted to can more, but I wasn't sure what the children would think of it. Now that I know the kids like it, I always make as much as I can. I looked at the various recipes for rhubarb juice that people in my church gave me and then just sort of made up my own. The cooked stalks make good compost for the garden.

8 pounds rhubarb, cut into 1-inch pieces

2 gallons water

2 (12-ounce) cans frozen orange juice

3 cups pineapple juice

4 cups sugar

1 (3-ounce) box strawberry-flavored gelatin

Combine the rhubarb and water in a large kettle on the stove and cook until the rhubarb is soft. Pour through a strainer and catch the rhubarb juice. Discard the cooked stalks. Add the orange juice, pineapple juice, sugar, and gelatin to the rhubarb juice. Stir until the sugar is dissolved. Pour the juice into sterilized jars and attach the seals and lids.

If you want to can and store the rhubarb juice, see page 81 for information on home canning.

RHUBARB CAKE DESSERT

Serves 4 to 6

This recipe reminds me of a rhubarb pie, just without the pie dough. This layered dessert is something that I usually make as a treat for the children in the spring. They seem to really like it.

CRUST

1 cup margarine or
   butter, softened

2 cups all-purpose flour

2 tablespoons sugar

TOPPING

6 large egg whites

Pinch of salt

¾ cup sugar

2 tablespoons vanilla extract

FILLING

6 large egg yolks

2 cups sugar

¼ cup all-purpose flour

¼ teaspoon salt

1 cup heavy cream or whole milk

5 cups rhubarb, cut into ½-inch pieces

Preheat the oven to 350°F. Butter the bottom and sides of a 9 by 13-inch cake pan.

To make the crust: Combine the margarine, flour, and sugar in a bowl and work until the mixture resembles coarse crumbs. Press evenly across the bottom of the cake pan.

To make the filling: Combine the egg yolks, sugar, flour, salt, and cream in a bowl. Stir until blended. Add the rhubarb and stir to incorporate. Pour the filling onto the crust. Bake until the filling is firm when you shake the pan a little, about 30 minutes. Remove from the oven, leaving the oven on, and let stand while making the topping.

To make the topping: Beat the egg whites and salt in a large bowl until soft peaks form. Gradually beat in the sugar until stiff, glossy peaks form. Fold in the vanilla until blended. Spread the topping evenly over the cake.

Return to the oven and bake until lightly browned, about 15 minutes. Remove from the oven and spoon into bowls or onto plates to serve.

RHUBARB DREAM BARS

Makes 15 bars

The sugar in this recipe takes the tartness out of the fruit, so even people who don't usually like rhubarb might like this!

CRUST

1½ cups all-purpose flour

⅔ cup powdered sugar

¼ cup margarine or butter, softened

FILLING

3 large eggs, beaten

2 cups sugar

½ cup all-purpose flour

½ teaspoon salt

3 cups chopped rhubarb

Preheat the oven to 350°F. Butter the bottom and sides of a 9 by 13-inch cake pan.

To make the crust: In a medium bowl, mix the flour, sugar, and margarine until the mixture resembles coarse crumbs. Press evenly across the bottom of the cake pan. Bake 15 minutes. Remove from the oven, leaving the oven on, and let stand while making the filling.

To make the filling: Combine the eggs, sugar, flour, and salt in a medium bowl. Stir to make a batter. Stir in the rhubarb until incorporated. Pour into the crust. Bake until the bars are firm when you shake the pan a little, about 35 minutes. Remove from the oven and let stand until completely cool. Cut into bars to serve.

RHUBARB COBBLER

Serves 6

This dish looks really nice when it is done, and it tastes great served with a scoop of ice cream!

TOPPING

1 cup all-purpose flour

2 tablespoons sugar

1½ teaspoons baking powder

¼ teaspoon salt

¼ cup margarine or butter

¼ cup milk

1 large egg, lightly beaten

FILLING

1 cup sugar

2 tablespoons cornstarch

¼ teaspoon ground cinnamon

4 cups rhubarb, chopped into 1-inch
 pieces

1 tablespoon water

1 tablespoon margarine or butter

Preheat the oven to 400°F. Butter the bottom and sides of an 8-inch-square baking dish.

To make the topping: Whisk the flour, sugar, baking powder, and salt in a medium bowl to blend. Rub in the margarine using your fingertips or cut it in with a pastry cutter until the mixture resembles coarse crumbs. Add the milk and egg, stirring just until incorporated.

To make the filling: Whisk the sugar, cornstarch, and cinnamon together in a medium saucepan. Stir in the rhubarb and water. Cook, stirring constantly, over medium heat until the mixture boils. Cook and stir 1 minute more.

Pour the filling into the prepared baking dish. Dot with the margarine. Immediately spoon the topping on the filling in 6 small mounds. Bake until the topping is golden brown, 20 to 25 minutes. Remove from the oven and serve warm.

SPRING CHICKEN

In the spring, we butcher our "broiler" chickens, the ones that will give us meat, like breasts, thighs, and legs. Butchering chickens is a messy job (see page 146), but we think it's worth the work for the delicious meat that we get from it.

PARMESAN CHICKEN
Serves 4 to 6

Here is an easy way to do chicken. This is another of Joe's favorites. There are many variations to this dish, but I'm sharing the recipe that probably makes it taste the best. I cook sometimes with just what I have on hand. For instance, if I am making this chicken and I don't have dried bread crumbs on hand, I'll use crackers in a pinch. Another thing I'll do if I don't have crumbs is just roll the chicken in corn flakes.

1 cup all-purpose flour

2 teaspoons salt

2 teaspoons sweet paprika

¼ teaspoon pepper

2 tablespoons garlic powder

2 large eggs

3 tablespoons milk

⅔ cup grated Parmesan cheese

⅓ cup dried bread crumbs

1 (3- to 4-pound) chicken, cut into serving pieces

Preheat the oven to 400°F.   Butter a 10 by 15-inch baking pan.

Combine the flour, salt, paprika, pepper, and garlic powder in a shallow bowl. Stir with a whisk to blend. Beat the eggs and milk in another shallow bowl. Combine the cheese and bread crumbs in a third shallow bowl. Dredge the chicken pieces in the flour mixture, then dip them into the egg mixture, then dredge them in the crumb mixture. Place in the prepared pan.

Bake until the juices run clear when a piece of chicken is pierced with a knife, 50 to 55 minutes.

EASY BAKED WHOLE CHICKEN

Serves 6 to 8

Our family loves to eat chicken this way. It is one of Joe's favorite ways for it to be served. I serve it with mashed potatoes and gravy since the children don't like rice (though it's good served cooked with rice, too). I also serve dressing with it (page 158).

1 (2- to 3-pound) chicken
1 (10¾-ounce) can of condensed cream of mushroom soup
½ cup milk
1 cup shredded Cheddar cheese
Salt and pepper

Preheat the oven to 350°F. Place the chicken in an 8-cup baking dish. Combine the soup, milk, and ½ cup of the cheese in a medium bowl. Stir to blend. Pour over the chicken and season with salt and pepper to taste. Cover the dish and bake for 60 minutes. Sprinkle the remaining ½ cup of cheese on top. Bake until the cheese is melted, about 15 minutes longer.

SPRING OUTSIDE OF THE KITCHEN

Of course spring isn't all about food; there are other events, both blessed and scary, that remind us of the season. Storms, weddings, taxes, and the end of the school year all remind us what time of year we are in.

In Indiana, and now here in Michigan, it seems spring always arrives with loud and destructive storms.

Storms

The weather in the spring can turn scary. We always fear tornadoes. I'm not sure if I've ever actually seen one. Once I saw a "tail" that I thought looked like a tornado. It was when we were in the buggy. It kind of dipped and went up again. I don't know if it was one. I hope I never see one. That is the closest I care to come.

The storm that scared me the most occurred shortly after we moved to Michigan. It was our first full day here and the rain and wind came and tore the neighbor-lady's shed roof off and uprooted a few of our trees. The neighbor-lady came over to warn us that there was a tornado coming our way, but we never saw one.

Another time, not long after we moved to Michigan, I was in the buggy with the children and it got really windy, began hailing, and the horse almost didn't want to keep going. While it was scary, it would have been worse being back in Indiana in a hailstorm while riding in the open buggy. We would have gotten battered with hail. I wear glasses, and in an open buggy the rain makes it almost impossible to see far away, especially when you have to take your glasses off. At least here in Michigan we are all closed in the buggy if a storm whips up. But the covered buggy tends to rock more in the wind, and that can be scary.

There is a prayer in our prayer book just for storms that we can say, and I remember Dad would recite it for us when such a time came. If it got really bad, we would all kneel down and pray together.

Prayer in time of heavy thunder and lightning

May God the Father, who hath no pleasure in our destruction, preserve us in life and death. May Jesus Christ, who is a Lord over life and death, rescue us also in this present peril. May God the Holy Spirit, our highest good, give us comfort, joy, and courage, so that we now and always may confidently rely on our God and not be too fearful of the weather, but be yielded to His will, thereupon also live penitently, henceforth be terrified of sin, diligently hear the voice of His Word, and engage our whole lives (in living up to it). Amen.

I know things are going to happen that are God's will, but I feel safer if I take the children down to the basement. They don't get as scared when they can't see anything. Usually, when the storms are really bad during the night I have them all come down and put beds on the floor, and they all feel better.

A lot of our children are scared when it starts thundering. They are worse since that storm that hit on our first full day here. If they hear thunder, they will come running in.

We don't have TV or radio, but sometimes you can just tell when a storm is about to blow up. If Joe sees a "sun dog" (a halo of reflective light near the sun), he says in three days the weather will change. He's always been interested in watching the moon and stars and figuring out how they relate to weather.

Understanding the weather helps make us less scared of it. My sisters Susan and Verena gave Joe a book about tornadoes for Christmas. And we gave daughter Susan one. The children really looked at that book a lot. Joe had to put it up in the bookcase because they had looked at it so much he didn't want them to ruin it. It really gave them an understanding of how bad a tornado could be.

We are in a rural area away from town, but my sister Emma and her husband, Jacob, live closer to the nearest village. I remember one time when we were at their house for supper. That night it looked really terrible outside, with the sky getting very black. We had the windows open and kept hearing the sirens. They are on the outskirts of town and can hear them. I am kind of glad we can't hear the sirens at our house, as they scare the children. We always tell the kids that God won't let anything happen that He doesn't want to.

WORSHIP AT HOME

A trait that distinguishes the Amish from their closely related Mennonite brethren is that the Amish worship in the homes of church members.

Church services usually begin around 9 A.M. and last about three hours. Services are held every other Sunday. Historically, however, the "every other week" worship has been done so Amish people could attend services in *other* districts. In theory, this keeps people from become too isolated in their own communities. Many Amish, however, just stay home and observe the Sabbath in a subdued, solemn manner rather than attend another service.

Services are held on a rotating basis among church members (excluding widows and young unmarrieds) so that everyone ends up taking a turn usually twice a year. Hosting a church service is a major event for the average Amish homemaker. She wants to make the best impression possible on her fellow church members. Usually, the whole house is cleaned and the family furnishes a full feast for the "after-church meal" that follows every service. This cookbook features many dishes that are traditionally offered after services. Such dishes vary from place to place, depending on local tradition.

Good Friday and Easter

If Easter falls on a Sunday that we are supposed to attend church services, then we will go to services on Easter morning. If Easter falls on a Sunday when we don't have church, then we will observe the day at home. Good Friday is usually when we have a quiet day to remember the death of Jesus on the cross. We keep that day to honor His suffering. We don't work on that day, and most all of the Amish in this area stay home from work. We fast and have a prayer day. In some other Amish communities, they work on that day just like any other.

Help me to also hold still, abstain from worldly, earthly business dealings, and rest from all false, unrepentant thought.

—Excerpt from prayer for Good Friday

During Easter weekend we tell our children the story of how Jesus died on the cross. And then just for something fun for the children, we color eggs. Growing up, we always had a bowl of colored eggs on Easter morning.

I usually buy dye for the eggs just because the color selection is better, but if I don't have dye, I use food coloring. White vinegar and food coloring will accomplish the same thing as dye. I usually like to color about ten dozen eggs so we can eat them over the Easter period. The children love hard-boiled eggs. They start eating them as soon as they start making them. Coloring the eggs can be quite messy. You can imagine six or seven children with dye on their hands, feet, and faces can be an ordeal to get cleaned up, but it is all good "clean" fun!

Ten dozen eggs may sound like a lot, but we use them up quickly in dandelion salads, which usually overlap with Easter. I don't like to risk keeping hard-boiled eggs around too long. The children will come home from school and the eggs will be their snack in the spring. Most of them love eggs and horseradish. Some of our children don't like horseradish, though, and they'll just put salt on the hard-boiled eggs.

We hide the eggs sometimes, just for fun. Usually, I buy a couple bags of plastic eggs and put little treats inside and we hide those. The children have fun taking turns hiding them, looking for them, and hiding them again.

Meal-wise, we don't really do anything different on Easter Sunday, except for our one Easter food tradition: enjoying the colored eggs along with homemade horseradish.

UNCLE SOLOMON'S HOMEMADE HORSERADISH
Makes 2 cups

Solomon is one of my husband Joe's favorite uncles who lives in Ohio. One year, he brought us horseradish root so we could try growing it ourselves. We had never tried growing our own up until that point. We tried it and really liked it. But keep in mind that once you plant it, it will spread, kind of like rhubarb does. It has become a favorite side dish to have with hard-boiled eggs in this household! Add additional salt and sugar to your own taste for this recipe.

1 (6- to 8-inch) piece horseradish root
½ cup distilled white vinegar
½ cup water

1 teaspoon sugar
Pinch of salt

Clean and very finely chop the horseradish root. Combine the vinegar, water, sugar, and salt in a small bowl, adding only enough horseradish to make it the thickness and spiciness you like. Cover and refrigerate until ready to serve.

EGG SALAD
Serves 20

Here is a great way to use up those leftover Easter eggs. This recipe is served at church a lot in place of ham salad, which is also a popular dish. It makes a great sandwich! Our children love this for sandwiches; they never get tired of it. This recipe is probably a bit large for the average family, so adjust it as needed.

6 pounds hot dogs
5 dozen eggs, hard-boiled (see page 33)
 and diced

6 cups Miracle Whip
2 cups mayonnaise
Salt and ground pepper

Grind the hot dogs in a meat grinder. In a large bowl, stir the ground meat, eggs, Miracle Whip, and mayonnaise together. Season to taste with salt and pepper. Cover and store in the refrigerator for up to three days.

Instructions for
the Perfect Hard-Boiled Egg

Getting an egg to cook just right through boiling isn't as easy as just throwing it in a pot of water. The timing is important; otherwise you could have an overcooked egg.

Someone at church gave me these instructions. This does always seem to make a great hard-boiled egg. The shells come right off, and the egg is cooked through perfectly.

Put the eggs in a pan of cold water. Bring to a boil, then cook for 2 minutes. Turn the heat off. Cover the pan and let stand for 11 minutes. Transfer the eggs to cold water and let them soak until cooled. Peel off the shells and enjoy.

APRIL 15: TAX DAY

One of the most common misconceptions about the Amish is that they are somehow exempt from paying taxes. Others believe that the Amish simply choose not to file and pay. I'm not sure where these misconceptions have their origins, because nothing is further from the truth. Certainly there are probably tax dodgers and evaders among the Amish—just as there are among the rest of us—but the vast majority pay their taxes without complaint. So April 15 is circled on many Amish calendars, just like any others.

Don't look for the Amish, though, to be using "E-file" or filing by telephone. Most still do their taxes the old-fashioned way: with paper, pencil, and a stamp. It is not uncommon, however, for Amish couples to use an outside "chain" tax preparer like H&R Block or a local non-Amish accountant.

Dan Bontrager—who is not Amish—runs a tax-preparing service in Kalona, Iowa, the state's largest and oldest Amish settlement. Year after year, he deals with an influx of Amish customers when the first tulips open their blooms in the April air. Bontrager and his staff make special provisions to deal with their Amish clients.

"We try to work around their schedules as best we can, since for them a trip into town might be an hour-long horse-drawn buggy ride. We think nothing of driving twenty or thirty miles for an appointment of any kind, but for our Amish customers even a five-mile trip is a bit of a journey," Bontrager says.

Just because Amish customers don't have QuickBooks or other fancy computer software to keep track of their expenses, though, doesn't mean that they aren't sophisticated in their monetary methods.

"I can't ever remember an Amish person coming into our office with a shoebox full of receipts. I cannot say the same for our non-Amish clients!" Bontrager adds that their record keeping is generally very thorough.

"Our more conservative Amish clients, of course, do all of their bookkeeping by hand. The records we see at the end of the year tend to be quite meticulous. As a general rule, their math is quite good and things are pretty well separated into various categories," Bontrager says.

The Amish will also use their often hidden humorous side to warm up the accountants.

"Iowa had a big ice storm that knocked out power to many families—some for a week or more. One of our more 'ornery' Amish clients came into our office and was complaining about not having any electricity to keep his goats warm. Then, with a smile, he exclaimed, "Oh yeah, I don't use electricity!" He also offered to put any of us up in his goat barn if we needed a warm place to stay for a while. We all got a laugh out of that."

Spring Cleaning

Those first sunny, 70-degree days in May definitely put us in a cleaning mood. We usually take one of the warm weekends in May to give our house a thorough spring cleaning after a winter spent mainly indoors.

One of the first things we do is take down all the curtains and give them a good washing. Our laundry lines will be full of fresh, clean curtains flapping in the breeze on an early weekend in May. While the curtains are down, we also wash all the windows and screens before putting them back on. Screens are kept in storage during the winter. So the screens are taken outside and hosed off.

Before we put the curtains back up, we wash all the walls and ceilings in the house with mops. The furniture is thoroughly cleaned, including taking the hickory rockers outside and spraying them down. We also take the mattresses and shake them out, dust them, and flip them over.

Once all the curtains are back on and the furniture washed down, I take everything out of my cabinets and wash them. This includes all the dishes, including the good ones that I hardly ever use.

Most of this cleaning is done when the children are home on spring break from school. My sisters also come over to help. If I am scheduled to have church services, say, in June or July, I might push back the cleaning schedule. Might as well do all that cleaning right before church.

It always feels so good to have everything clean again. With eight children's dirty little hands around the house, things can get smudged up really quickly, but, at least after spring cleaning, everything shines again for awhile. The children all seem to enjoy pitching in, so it really is good family time together.

Lovina's thoughts on tax time:

I always loved math and was always good at it. I don't know the rules of what you have to figure and stuff as related to taxes, so Joe and I always go to a tax preparer.

There are tax preparers who are members of the Amish faith, which some use. Mom and Dad used to have an Amish man do theirs, but with all the tax-rule changes they switched to H&R Block. A lot of the Amish use H&R Block. For us, tax time is a good thing, because we get a refund as Joe has the taxes taken out the whole year.

Verena, age 9, her view of the family.

Mother's Day

I think it depends on the family: Some Amish observe Mother's Day, others don't. We've always marked the day in some way. We married children would always get Mom a plant or another small gift. One year for Mother's Day, my children got me two potted flowers. Another year, they went and took a big poster board, and they all had a section on it, and they all wrote a poem or whatever they wanted in their section.

A lot of times the teachers in school will have the children make cards or draw pictures for their mothers.

One year, Loretta gave me a flower. Another time, Verena gave me a cucumber plant. I put both of them in the garden. The cucumber plant produced pickles, and Verena was so thrilled when I showed her the bounty that came off her plant. One year, Benjamin came home with a cup of soil with a tiny plant in it. He thought it was a weed and pulled it; he later kind of wished he hadn't when he saw the plants his sister brought home, because those were put out into the garden where they really grew.

As a mother, disciplining children is the hardest thing. It almost breaks your heart to have to punish them. When I was a girl living at home my brothers and sisters and I always knew we could get by with more with Dad. Dad would say yes and give in quicker. My kids seem to listen more to Joe. When Lovina would have a fit at church, for instance, all Joe would have to do is take her outside and talk with her and she'd straighten up.

I always thought it would be nice to have a big family. We were only eight children at home. Among the Amish eight isn't considered a big family—fifteen or sixteen children is a big family.

I always thought I'd like to have twelve. I'd go overnight to my friend's house and they'd have a lot more children than us. They could make kickball teams out of all the brothers and sisters. You can do a lot more things with a big family.

What I do miss is not having Mom around as I raise my children. For the first six children Mom was there for every childbirth. I missed that when I had Lovina and Kevin. It was a comfort to have her there.

After Mother's Day, the danger of frost disappears and the garden gets in gear.

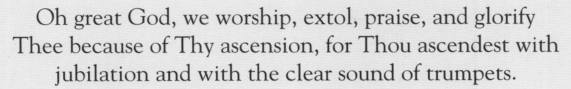

ASCENSION DAY: 40 DAYS AFTER EASTER

Oh great God, we worship, extol, praise, and glorify
Thee because of Thy ascension, for Thou ascendest with
jubilation and with the clear sound of trumpets.

—Amish prayer for Ascension Day

Many church denominations are built around a centralized administrative structure, whether it is the Roman Catholic Church's Vatican headquarters or the Latter-Day Saints' Salt Lake City authority. The Amish church, however, lacks such a central structure. There is no singular person or entity that runs the day-to-day business of the church on a national or even regional level. There have been attempts at loose structural elements, such as a steering committee of Amish bishops that meets annually or biannually to discuss church direction. But such efforts haven't resulted in any formal church structure. This lack of centralization can cause considerable differences in doctrine and customs from church district to church district. For instance, one Amish church district may allow its members to have indoor plumbing, while a neighboring one will not. The local bishop is given wide latitude to determine church direction.

The differences among Amish churches manifest themselves even on the religious calendar. Some Amish churches observe Ascension Day, while others do not. Ascension Day is the celebration of Christ's resurrection into heaven and is observed forty days after Easter Sunday.

In Berne, Indiana's Amish community, for example, the day is little noted by the church, with people going about their business as usual. In northern Indiana's large Amish settlements, Ascension Day is marked by fasting, prayer, and spending quiet time with family. A large portion of the men living in northern Indiana's Amish community are employed by local factories. Factories with large numbers of Amish employees are forced to close on Ascension Day each year because so many workers stay home.

The Eichers are typical of many Amish families in communities where Ascension Day is observed. The morning is spent in prayer and fasting, followed by an evening of feasting and fellowship. It's become a good day to pause from the bustle of spring planting and end-of-school-term homework.

SPRING GARDEN GOODIES

A lot goes into making a successful garden. There are flowers along the border, usually marigolds and zinnias. The marigolds are good for mole prevention. We always do a marigold border around the garden.

Vegetables we plant: peas, green onions, sweet onions, radishes, three or four kinds of lettuce, carrots, celery, red beets, sweet corn, green beans, tomatoes, green peppers, hot peppers, chili peppers, zucchinis, cabbage, endive, turnips, winter radishes, cucumbers, strawberries, watermelons, and pumpkins, if space permits.

PEAS

We plant a lot of fresh peas. The children will eat them raw with salt. They'll go out and get quite a few pods of peas and just snack on them. We like them in salads and also in vegetable soups. The children like only fresh peas right out of the garden or frozen peas, but they don't care for the canned peas, home canned or store-bought. Peas take a lot of time when you can them because of all the little peas you have to wash. I've tried growing and canning quite a few different varieties.

We either eat them raw or just cook them in water. One funny thing that I remember about peas is that my daughter Elizabeth would eat corn but never eat peas. My sister Liz babysat for her one day. After I picked Elizabeth up, on the way home I asked her what she had for lunch. She said "Aunt Liz served me green corn; it was gross and green." Turns out it was creamed peas, which she had never heard of before, but she had heard of creamed corn so she thought it was that.

Although our children would rather eat peas raw instead of cooked, I don't care for them raw. My daughter Verena likes peas the most. She'll ask if she can have them for her birthday. But I tell her that in December there won't be any fresh peas. Verena is another one who doesn't like canned peas. She was so glad once when Aunt Emma had peas on the table, so she took a big helping, put some in her mouth, and asked, "What is wrong with these peas?" Turns out they were home-canned peas. I think they don't like them canned because they are mushier; the canned peas don't have the crunch to them.

Peas, green onions, and radishes are the first to harvest, although potatoes can sometimes come up really early if the weather cooperates. Some people have potatoes ready to plant by Good Friday.

We love to eat those first peas when they come out of the garden. We find uses for them in soups, casseroles, and as a side dish.

HAM AND PEA SALAD

Serves 6 to 8

This is just such an easy way to use fresh peas from the garden. This salad is very colorful and is a favorite to serve to people after church services.

2 cups green peas
1½ cups chopped cooked ham
1 cup shredded Cheddar cheese
1 cup chopped red onion
½ cup ranch salad dressing

In a serving bowl, combine the peas, ham, cheese, and onion. Pour the dressing over the top and toss to coat evenly.

FRESH PEA SALAD

Serves 4 to 6

This salad is a favorite among my children because they all seem to love raw peas so much. I wish they were in season in December so I could fix this for Verena's birthday!

1 cup green peas
½ cup sweet pickle relish
½ cup chopped onion
½ cup shredded Colby or Cheddar cheese
6 hard-boiled eggs (see page 33), chopped
¾ cup mayonnaise or Miracle Whip salad dressing

Cook the peas in salted boiling water until tender, 7 to 10 minutes. Drain and let cool. Transfer to a medium bowl and stir all the remaining ingredients into the peas. Cover and chill before serving.

BEETS

Red beets also make for good early eats from the garden. We enjoy them pickled. Beets don't get as much attention from us as some of the other vegetables, because we just don't fix them in too many different ways. Adding them to different dishes will give a bright red color, which sometimes isn't the most appetizing. Beets are easy to grow, though, so I always make sure several rows are planted.

PICKLED RED BEETS

Makes 8 quarts

We fix these mostly around when we have church, although sometimes I'll just open a quart jar for us to eat and enjoy as a family. Sometimes the children will eat beets just like a snack, but church is mostly where we have them. Almost everyone seems to serve pickled beets after church services. Sometimes the food served after services will be different from place to place, but the one thing that doesn't seem to change is the pickled beets. They can be prepared a lot of different ways, so I always taste one when I am visiting someplace to make sure I like them! This is our favorite way to fix them. I prepared the amounts for this recipe the best I could using medium-sized beets. You may need to prepare more "pickling juice" to ensure the beets are covered.

10 large (softball-sized) beets, diced into 1-inch cubes

4 cups sugar

4 cups water

4 cups apple cider vinegar

2 teaspoons salt

2 teaspoons pickling spice

Fill a large nonaluminum pot three-fourths full with water. Bring to a boil over medium-high heat, add the beets, and cook until tender, 1 to 1½ hours. Beets take a long time to cook. Be sure to add water as it evaporates so the beets are always covered. Drain the beets, let them cool, then peel off the skin. Set the beets aside and prepare the pickling juice.

In a large nonaluminum saucepan, combine the sugar, water, vinegar, salt, and pickling spice. Bring to a boil over medium-high heat and add the beets; make sure they are covered with liquid. Cook for 5 to 10 minutes and then put into sterilized jars and seal.

If you want to can and store the beets, see page 81 for more information on home canning.

RADISHES

Now we move on to a real treat, though not everyone likes them: radishes.

Radishes are always one of the things we have on the table in the spring. Radishes, green onions, and lettuce are the first three things out of the garden for us, and we really enjoy them.

The first radishes in the spring are the best ones. I plant them shortly after the danger of the first frost is over, and they always surprise me by how quickly they begin to grow. I take them out when they are marble-sized, because I am so hungry for a bite after a long winter without them. Some gardeners around here, if the weather cooperates, have radishes as soon as April.

Radishes are a healthful snack for the children, and something they really enjoy. Our favorite way to eat them is either in a salad or simply sliced and salted. The children will eat them anytime; in fact, my youngest, Lovina and Kevin, will sit there and eat them while I am washing them.

Another way we eat them is with butter and bread as a sandwich. Mom would have that as her lunch many times. That is a meal that my daughter Susan has also taken a liking to, and it's neat to see her taking after her grandma.

The timing of when you plant and harvest your radishes really determines the taste. When the weather is nice and cool, the radishes don't taste spicy. Once the weather gets hot, the radishes get hotter and spicier. I think the sun does that to them. There is also a big difference in taste between the radishes you buy in stores and the ones you get from the garden. The ones from the garden are crisper. But you have to pick them early. Once they start seeding, they get harder to eat and they aren't good anymore. So, radishes are mainly a spring-to-early-summer treat, although you can plant some in July or maybe August and have them in the fall as a winter radish. Then they taste more like a turnip.

Radish seeds are tiny, so I plant rows and rows and rows of them. I put some into the garden and then, a little later on, maybe a week or two later, I'll plant more. That way they will not all be ready at the same time and we can enjoy them longer.

One more thing about radishes: They don't freeze well and you can't really can them. So just enjoy them while you can!

GARDEN RADISH SALAD

Serves 6 to 8

I rarely buy radishes in the stores; they just don't taste as good. But since their growing season is so short and they don't keep very well, I will sometimes buy them at a supermarket if we want to have them in a salad other times of the year.

4 cups radishes, trimmed and sliced

½ cup thinly sliced onion

1 cup diced tomatoes

1¼ teaspoons salt

1 small clove garlic, minced

⅛ teaspoon freshly ground pepper

1 teaspoon minced fresh basil or mint

2 tablespoons fresh lemon juice

2 tablespoons olive oil

Minced fresh parsley for garnish

Combine the radishes, onion, and tomatoes in a bowl. In a separate bowl, whisk together the salt, garlic, pepper, basil, lemon juice, and oil. Toss the dressing with the salad and then garnish with the parsley.

HOMEMADE RADISH RELISH

Makes 2 pints

This makes for a different, tangy, and tasty relish to put on hot dogs, to eat with pork chops, or to serve alongside fish.

1 pound radishes, trimmed and sliced

1 onion, cut into thin strips

2 tablespoons allspice berries

¼ teaspoon whole cloves

1 teaspoon mustard seeds

1 cup distilled white vinegar

¾ cup sugar

½ teaspoon salt

¾ cup water

Combine the radishes and onion in a large stainless-steel bowl. Toss to blend and set aside.

Make a spice bag by tying the allspice, cloves, and mustard seeds in a square of cheesecloth. Place the bag in a large nonaluminum saucepan and add the vinegar, sugar, salt, and water. Bring the mixture to a boil, then reduce the heat to a simmer, cover, and cook for 5 minutes. Uncover and cook for 10 minutes. Pour the hot liquid over the radishes in the bowl. Let stand for 15 minutes. Use now, or pour the relish into a clean pint jar and let cool slightly. Cap the jar and refrigerate for up to 2 weeks.

STRAWBERRIES

With their bright red bursts of color and sweet juiciness, strawberries are always welcome once they begin to offer themselves from the earth. Our yard becomes our grocery store every spring as strawberries add to the list of goodies we can begin to harvest.

STRAWBERRY PIE

Serves 6 to 8

This recipe is one of the first cool, delicious desserts we whip up on warm days. My sister Susan is especially fond of making this, and it doesn't last very long when she brings it over!

CRUST
1½ cups all-purpose flour
½ teaspoon salt
½ cup vegetable oil
2 tablespoons milk
2 tablespoons sugar

FILLING
½ cup sugar
3 tablespoons cornstarch
2 tablespoons light corn syrup
1 cup water
3 tablespoons strawberry-flavored gelatin
Few drops of red food coloring (optional)
6 cups fresh strawberries, hulled and sliced

To make the crust: Preheat the oven to 400°F. Stir together the flour, salt, oil, milk, and sugar in a medium bowl. Press the dough evenly over the bottom and up the sides of a 9-inch pie pan. Bake until golden, about 12 minutes. Remove from the oven and let cool.

To make the filling: Combine the sugar, cornstarch, corn syrup, and water in a saucepan and bring to a boil. Boil, stirring constantly, until thick, about 5 minutes. Remove from the heat. Stir in the gelatin and food coloring. Let cool until lukewarm. Add the strawberries and pour into the cooled crust. Refrigerate for 2 hours before serving.

PANCAKES WITH FRESH STRAWBERRIES
Serves 4 to 6

This is a recipe that the kids like on a spring morning. It is easy to go out and pick the strawberries from the garden patch and bring them in for a pancake breakfast. Delicious!

BATTER

2 cups all-purpose flour

1 tablespoon plus ½ teaspoon baking powder

½ teaspoon salt

1⅓ cups milk

2 tablespoons vegetable oil, plus more for cooking the pancakes

1 tablespoon vanilla extract

1 egg, beaten

Strawberries

Sweetened whipped cream for garnish

To make the batter: Combine the flour, baking powder, and salt in a medium bowl. Stir with a whisk to blend. In another bowl, whisk the milk, oil, vanilla, and egg together. Stir the wet ingredients into the dry ingredients just until combined; do not overmix.

Put a little oil on a griddle or in a large skillet and heat over medium-high heat. Drop the batter by tablespoons onto the griddle or in the pan to form several small pancakes. Cook until golden on each side, 2 to 3 minutes. Transfer the pancakes to plates. Top the pancakes with a few strawberries and some whipped cream.

Play mirrors reality for many Amish children. Games that imitate real-life situations like "school" or "farmer" are a fun way that Amish children prepare for adult life.

STARTING FROM SCRATCH

With a church doctrine that prohibits birth control, Amish families are predictably large. When you combine big families with a culture that still makes an attempt at agrarianism (you won't find Amish families living in the Bronx or suburban Chicago), you can end up with land shortages in some settlements. Lancaster County, Pennsylvania, was once home to the largest population of Amish in the United States. Holmes County, Ohio, has since surpassed its Keystone neighbor, but Amish populations in Pennsylvania still have limited room to grow. One solution is simply to move someplace far away and start a settlement from scratch. Late spring is a good time to journey to a new destination, so that families can have the summer to settle in before the arrival of a new school year.

Some Amish in Lancaster County have chosen in recent years to get away from the tourism, the crowded roads, and the "big box" stores creeping their way from suburban Philadelphia's outer fringes. The early- to mid-1990s witnessed waves of Amish leaving Lancaster County. A large group moved to Christian County, Kentucky, while a smaller contingent chose Parke County, Indiana.

Prior to 1990, Parke County was best known for its thirty-one covered bridges dotting the county countryside. The county still bills itself as the "Covered Bridge Capital of the World." With only 16,000 full-time residents, the county is an outpost along I-70 between Indianapolis and Saint Louis. This is just the kind of rural character that Amish looking to establish new roots find appealing.

"I was contacted by a former Amish man who lived in Pennsylvania. He still had close relationships with the Amish in Lancaster County," remembers George Waltz, at the time the county extension agent for Parke County. "He knew that they were getting crowded by urbanization, and they also crowd themselves with big families."

Waltz suddenly found himself in the middle of assisting a large migration from Lancaster County.

"Farming is their first occupation. Every so often they'll want to migrate someplace where it is not so crowded. Parke County is quite rural, with average or above farmland. A lot of them have dairy cows and like rolling land. Parke County is not a congested area, and the land is pretty good." Waltz says. Indiana's large Amish settlements also were a factor. While there were no Amish in the Parke County area, locals still had at least passing familiarity with "plain people." "They wanted a place where they would be accepted," Waltz said.

Waltz was set to retire soon from the extension agent job, which he had held for twenty-seven years. On retirement, Waltz worked with new Amish families as a Realtor for a while. He helped around twenty families settle into the Parke County area.

In some areas where Amish move in for the first time, there can be tension. Anything from the horse droppings on public roads to the false perception that the Amish don't pay taxes has caused problems in other communities. Parke County, however, rolled out the welcome mat, thanks largely to Waltz.

"I called a meeting of community citizens about the time they wanted to come here. There was never any major opposition to begin with, but that meeting helped a lot," Waltz said. The heads of various organizations were invited along with a couple of Amish.

Almost twenty years later, the Parke County settlement is thriving.

"They filled a niche. They are a good, moral, hardworking people," Waltz says. The Parke County Amish population now stands at around one hundred families in several church districts.

Today, one-room schoolhouses dot the countryside. And several small produce businesses, bakeries, furniture shops, and horseshoeing operations have opened, creating an economic benefit for everyone. This doesn't surprise Waltz.

"When you know them a little bit, it is fair to say they are just like everybody else," Waltz says.

The Amish can sometimes be described as seminomadic, often moving from place to place to find the best farmland or to leave behind growing suburbia. Sometimes, whole church communities uproot and leave, other times it is simply a single family or two leaving. The Eichers, as is typical for the Amish, decided to leave behind their Indiana roots in 2004 to settle closer to Joe's family in Michigan. While the move was an adjustment, they've been quite happy with the decision.

Once the "spring migration" and moves are completed, the garden tilled, and the last of the schoolwork finished for the term, Amish families turn their attention to summer, a slow-paced season of much work and much fun.

summer

Guard us, Lord Christ, all together, from fire, hail, and thunderclaps. Protect all who are in the field so that the storm does not set them on fire. Preserve cattle, men, and grain. Then young and old will praise and glorify Thee.

—Amish prayer

Summer is a special time of hard work, but also a lot of fun.

There are days spent at the fishing lake, the children outside having water fights, and daylight late in the evening. The later light saves us from using those hot gas lamps indoors as much. During July and August, a lot of our days are spent outside, and that is what makes summer such a favorite season around here. The area of Michigan that we live in is full of apple orchards that begin to send out a fragrant scent in summer. And unlike the cold winter months, when laundry is dried indoors and takes longer, summer is when clothing can be washed, dried, folded, and put away in a single day. And along with summer comes gardening, canning, and the harvesting of hay. The wonderful smell of fresh vegetables from the garden fills our house at suppertime. The season also reminds me of the taste of those delicious tomatoes and the first bites of sweet corn.

Also, in the summer, evenings are more relaxed: no nights spent helping the children with seemingly endless piles of homework from school, rushing to get supper on the table, and then getting the children off to bed early. Having the children home and not rushing around in the morning to get them off to school makes this season different from the rush of the others. We get to sleep in an extra hour in the summer when the children are home. So there is just a more relaxed feel to the season, even though there is also much work to be done.

Summer brings hay season, with our first cutting usually in July. And even though it is a hot job to unload the wagons, we are glad to fill our barns with fresh hay. We use it to feed our horses through the winter months.

FATHER'S DAY
by Joe Eicher

I always enjoy a good meal with my family. It is a good time for us all to be together. During the summer, we always enjoy more outdoor snacks. Sometimes we will roast marshmallows and hot dogs over an open fire. It's a good time spent together with the family.

I also like taking the boys mushroom hunting and fishing and look forward to them being old enough to someday take deer hunting. The joys of being a father far outweigh anything bad. One of the highlights is coming home from work and seeing the children run out to meet me. I like standing outside in the driveway with my hands outstretched and having the children race. Whoever tags my hand first at the finish line is the winner. Another good memory is when the older girls have warm cookies baked or something for a treat when I get home.

I like to go bike riding with all my children. I always look forward to seeing them open a birthday gift or blowing the candles out on their cake. And then I enjoy helping them put a Christmas gift together so they can play with it. Another fatherhood favorite is listening to our children sing songs, and I enjoy having them come out and help with chores.

It's also fun to play kickball and basketball with them. And we like the game Andy-Over, which involves throwing a ball back and forth over the house. Another game we like to play is kick the can. I try to pass on things I learned from my father to my children. I learned the carpenter trade from my father, as well as how to lay bricks, how to make rabbit cages, and how to deer hunt.

My father was always good with preparing meats on the grill, and I like to cook on the grill also. Meat cooked on an outdoor grill always tastes great during the summer. We can cook deer steaks or hamburgers. The men also do a lot of the most difficult work in butchering our meat, and our wives are always appreciative of that.

Kevin's note: The summer starts out with a celebration of food and fathers. While people think of Amish women as working in the kitchen, men play an important role in getting meals on the table, too.

SUMMER GARDEN GOODIES

The warm days of late June, July, and August bring hot peppers, zucchinis, squash, green peppers, cucumbers, and potatoes. We do grow some green beans each summer also. Maybe I will plant one good long row of them, perhaps about fifteen plants. I usually plant the "slender-ette" kind. My children like them cooked with a can of cream of mushroom soup and crumbled bacon mixed in. We also like them in a vegetable soup (see Grandma's Soup on page 99) and sometimes add them to homemade vegetable juice (page 80).

Our garden efforts are focused most on the vegetables that our family really likes: Onions, tomatoes, corn, and zucchini are particular favorites.

By early August, tomatoes and corn are ready, although I've had corn by July 14 before. It just depends on how early the garden was planted and when the first frost comes.

ONIONS

As far as onions go, I always make sure I plant "cooking onions," which are the yellow ones. These are good in stews, soups, and meats. Then I also plant sweet onions, which we like sliced on sandwiches. I buy the "candy onions" or "Spanish" ones. We seem to like the taste of both. But I don't use the same kinds each year; it just depends on what the local Amish-owned greenhouse is offering for sale.

I always make sure my onions are out of the ground by August 1. My mother always said don't let the August sun hit them. I think she meant that if the warm sun beats down on them too long that they will begin rotting. So we make sure our onions are picked by the end of July, and we hang them up on strings in our cellar and dry them. Sometimes, we even let them hang somewhere in the shed for a while. However a person chooses to hang them, once they are moisture-free, you lay them out on newspapers and tie them off. Most years I don't have to buy any onions from the store, because we have enough to last from season to season. If we run out, I'll just use fresh green onions in the spring.

ONION PIE

Serves 4 to 6

This is a recipe that even people who don't care for onions will probably like. It's a good way to use up those extra onions from the garden!

4 slices bacon

2 cups chopped onions

2 large eggs, beaten

1 cup sour cream

1 tablespoon all-purpose flour

½ teaspoon salt

¼ teaspoon ground pepper

1 disk My Homemade Pie Dough (page 125)

Preheat the oven to 400°F. Fry the bacon in a skillet until crisp. Transfer the bacon to paper towels to drain. Drain most of the fat from the pan, leaving just enough to coat the bottom of the skillet. Add the onions and sauté until translucent, about 3 minutes. Remove from the heat and let cool.

Whisk the eggs and sour cream together in a small bowl. Whisk in the flour, then the salt and pepper.

Roll out the disk of dough to a ⅛-inch thickness on a floured surface. Fit into a 9-inch pie pan and trim to a 1-inch overhang. Fold the dough under and crimp the edges. Using a fork, prick several holes in the bottom of the crust. Spread the onion and bacon over the bottom of the pie shell. Pour in the filling. Bake for 15 minutes. Lower the oven temperature to 350°F and bake for another 15 minutes, or until nicely browned. Remove from the oven. Cut into wedges and serve hot.

ZUCCHINI

When the zucchinis are ripe, usually by late July or early August, it is a sure sign we are in the middle of summer. Zucchini wasn't something our family always ate, but once we started it quickly became a family favorite. I remember one time I decided to introduce my children to zucchini by frying it into patties. I didn't really think they'd like them. But before the platter got around I had to get up quickly and fry up another batch! We've all been hooked ever since.

We've had a bit more difficulty growing zucchini in Michigan than in Indiana. In Indiana, it was one of the easiest things to grow. I think it has something to do with the bugs that are here in Michigan. Zucchinis seem more difficult to grow here past midsummer. Cucumbers are the same. I like zucchinis best when they are smaller. When they get bigger they have more seeds, which are more work to take out. And, besides, they deep-fry better when smaller.

Zucchini can be used in so many different ways. Some people try to cut down on the amount of bread and potatoes in their diet. For those people, zucchini can be used as an alternative. For instance, I have found that zucchini can be used as an easy substitute for potatoes. When I do a casserole, I now use zucchini in place of potatoes. The zucchinis will do the same thing; you can hardly tell the difference in taste. Even when a recipe for calls for hashed brown potatoes, I will use grated zucchini instead. It's impossible to tell the difference, I think. Zucchinis can also be used to make jams, breads, and soups. There is not much you can't do with zucchini, which is why we always look forward to its arrival.

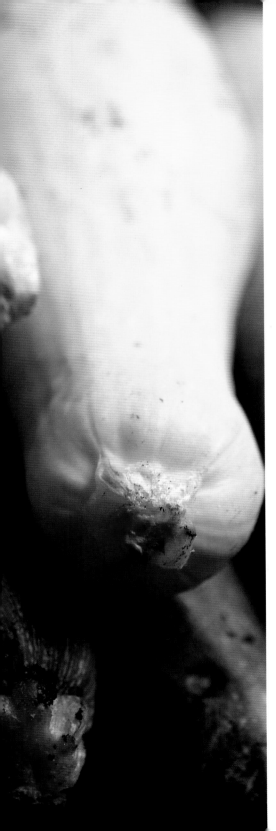

ZUCCHINI CASSEROLE

Serves 4 to 6

This casserole is great as a main dish for supper. If you want a meatless dish, this tastes great even without the ground beef.

1 pound ground beef

1 (1¼-ounce) package taco seasoning

4 large eggs

½ cup olive oil

½ teaspoon salt

½ teaspoon ground pepper

1 teaspoon minced fresh parsley (optional)

3 cups shredded zucchini

1 cup Bisquick

¼ cup shredded onion

½ cup shredded cheese, any kind

Preheat the oven to 350°F. Grease a 9 by 13-inch baking dish.

Brown the ground beef in a large skillet and stir in the taco seasoning. Drain and set aside.

Beat the eggs, oil, salt, pepper, and parsley together in a large bowl until blended. Stir in the zucchini, Bisquick, and onion until smooth. Stir in the ground beef until distributed evenly in the mixture. Pour into the prepared dish. Bake for 30 minutes, then sprinkle evenly with the cheese. Continue baking until the cheese is melted, about 10 minutes. Remove from the oven and spoon onto individual plates to serve.

ZUCCHINI PATTIES

Serves 4 to 6

This is a great way to get rid of excess zucchini. In addition to just eating these as patties, we also like to eat them in a sandwich, with lettuce, tomato, and onions piled on. Some people add oats or bread crumbs to the mixture, but I've found that everything holds together very well this way. During zucchini season, this recipe will often be our main supper dish. We might serve some fresh corn on the side or perhaps some beets and sliced bread. But this alone makes for a great supper!

3 tablespoons olive oil

3 cups peeled and shredded zucchini

3 large eggs

1 cup shredded Cheddar cheese

Salt

8 to 10 slices Velveeta cheese (optional)

Heat the oil in a large skillet over medium-high heat. Stir the zucchini, eggs, Cheddar cheese, and salt to taste together in a large bowl. Drop the batter by tablespoons into the skillet pan. As the batter begins to thicken, shape it into patties using a metal spatula and fry until golden brown, about 3 minutes on each side.

Top with a slice of Velveeta and serve.

ZUCCHINI RELISH
Makes 6 to 7 pints

*This relish is a delicious spread for sandwiches. You can use it just like a pickle relish. After church, when we have so many sandwiches to serve it is a nice thing to offer people. Even though the recipe calls for jalapenos, just two in this big of a batch won't do much more than just give it a little flavor. The relish is mild enough that kids can eat and enjoy it. More peppers can be added if you want that flavor. (***Note:*** This recipe needs to be started the day before you serve the relish.)*

10 cups peeled and grated zucchini

4 cups chopped yellow onion

5 tablespoons salt

2¼ cups distilled white vinegar

3 cups sugar

1 teaspoon ground nutmeg

3 medium green bell peppers, seeded and ground in a food processor (about 2 cups)

1 teaspoon ground turmeric

2 teaspoons dry mustard

½ teaspoon celery salt

2 small jalapeno peppers

Combine the zucchini, onion, and salt in a medium bowl. Cover and let stand overnight.

The next morning, rinse the zucchini mixture in cold water and drain. Set aside.

Combine the vinegar, sugar, nutmeg, green peppers, turmeric, mustard, celery salt, and jalapenos in a large bowl. Stir in the zucchini mixture. Pour it all into a large stockpot and bring it just to a boil over high heat. Reduce the heat to low and simmer for 30 minutes.

Put the relish into sterilized pint jars and seal.

If you want to can the zucchini relish, see page 81 for more information on home canning.

ZUCCHINI JAM

Makes 4 pints

I remember that the first time I tried this jam it was hard to believe it was zucchini because it tasted nice and sweet. Often I think of zucchini as something to eat at supper, not to spread on bread for breakfast! I think the sugar in the recipe really hides the taste of the zucchini. This is a great spread for toast and other breads. It's sometimes served during the meal after church in place of other jams.

6 cups peeled and shredded zucchini

1 cup water

6 cups sugar

2 tablespoons fresh lemon juice

1 (20-ounce) can crushed pineapple

2 (3-ounce) boxes apricot-flavored gelatin

Combine the zucchini and water in a small saucepan and bring to a boil over medium heat. Reduce the heat to low and cook for 6 minutes. Stir in the sugar, lemon juice, and pineapple. Bring to a boil again and cook for 6 minutes more. Add the gelatin and mix well. Immediately pour into sterilized pint jars and attach the seals and lids. The heat will seal the jars.

Note: See page 81 for more information on home canning.

ZUCCHINI BARS

Makes 40 bars

This is a favorite in some Amish homes around here. Our children like brownies or any kind of bars, so these seem to go over well in our home!

2½ cups all-purpose flour

1 cup whole-wheat flour

2 teaspoons baking soda

1½ teaspoons salt

2 teaspoons ground cinnamon

2 cups sugar

1 cup vegetable oil

4 eggs, beaten

⅔ cup water

2 cups peeled and grated zucchini

1 (12-ounce) package chocolate chips

1 (12-ounce) package butterscotch chips

1 cup chopped walnuts (optional)

Preheat the oven to 350°F. Grease two 9 by 13-inch baking pans or one 12 by 17-inch baking pan.

    Combine the flours, baking soda, salt, cinnamon, and sugar in a large bowl and stir with a whisk to blend. Add the oil, eggs, and water and stir until smooth. Stir in all the remaining ingredients. Stir for about 5 minutes until everything is very evenly blended. Then pour the batter into the prepared pan(s). Bake for 35 minutes, or until firm. Remove from the oven, let cool, and cut into squares.

Getting the Children to Eat Their Vegetables

Having eight children, it can be a challenge to get them all to try new things. I've learned, though, as I've gone along how to get my children to enjoy their vegetables. With my oldest child, I'd never really have her try different things and now she is my pickiest eater. I learned from this. When the younger ones came along, I would have them try eating everything and now they aren't so picky.

Some of the children try new foods earlier than others. Elizabeth used to not like cucumbers but as she has gotten older I see a difference. If the children see a particular food on the table all the time they kind of get used to it and try it. Another trick is to serve foods to Joe. One reason the children started eating salad was that I would always fix Joe a salad, he'd give them a bite out of his, and they'd like it. Now, they almost all eat salads.

One of my daughters Susan and Verena's favorite places in the garden is the pea patch. They will go out there with a salt shaker, open up some pods, and eat them right there.

The children don't care for green beans yet, but I cream them and dice them a little smaller, and they like them. Or if there is something from the garden I want them to have, I will put it into a vegetable soup and smash crackers over it. They never know what they are eating.

CUCUMBERS

We put out about a dozen cucumber plants each summer. I have always had luck with mine.

Cucumbers grow on vines, so you have to plan accordingly space-wise in the garden. I like what are called "straight eight" cucumbers, which are very firm and crisp for slicing. They are also good to use for making sweet and sour pickles. A variety called Market More is another that I like to plant, as the cucumbers do not get bitter in the hot sun. The most important thing for me is to choose one that won't get too big. I like to choose cucumbers that will stay slender and small, not as wide. A fatter, plumper cucumber usually has more seeds, which makes it more difficult to cook with.

One way we enjoy eating cucumbers is just by slicing them and putting salt on them. That is really our favorite way to eat them. Sometimes, I take salad dressing and make a cucumber salad, but we eat them just with salt most of the time.

FREEZER PICKLES

Makes about 4 pints

I store these in large containers in the freezer so when I have church I can serve them for the meal afterward. But I can also freeze them in smaller containers so we can eat them at home on sandwiches. It is really surprising how crisp they are. These pickles will stay good in the freezer for up to a year. They taste so fresh and crunchy. The making of these pickles does stretch out over three days, so plan accordingly!

4 to 5 cucumbers, peeled and cut into ½-inch-thick slices
2 tablespoons salt
1 large onion, sliced
1¾ cups sugar
½ cup distilled white vinegar

Day 1: Put the cucumbers, salt, and onion in a large bowl. Cover and refrigerate for 24 hours.

Day 2: Drain the juice from the cucumbers. Combine the sugar and vinegar and stir to dissolve the sugar. Pour the mixture over the cucumbers. Cover and refrigerate for 24 hours.

Day 3: Take the pickles out of refrigerator and pack into a freezer-safe container(s). Pour the syrup over the pickles and freeze until ready to use.

SWEET AND SOUR GARLIC DILL PICKLES
Makes 2 quarts

These pickles are slightly tangy, and they add a really good flavor to a meat sandwich. They are almost always served at the meal after church. I slice these the long way. Most of my children like them. My daughter Susan, for instance, will open a jar and make herself a peanut butter and pickle sandwich. I keep the skins on my cucumbers for this recipe, but you can do it to suit your preference.

2 cups water
2 cups distilled white vinegar
3 cups sugar
2 tablespoons salt
4 to 6 cucumbers, cut into ½-inch-thick spears
⅛ teaspoon garlic powder or 1 clove fresh garlic
1 teaspoon minced fresh dill

Bring the water, vinegar, sugar, and salt to a boil in a small nonaluminum saucepan.

Divide the garlic and dill into 4 even portions and place in the bottom of each of 4 sterilized pint jars. Put the cucumbers into the jars, pour the vinegar mixture over them, and seal the jars. Process the jars of pickles according to the instructions on page 81.

THE BUGGY

For the Eichers, as is the case for most all Amish, the horse-drawn buggy is the primary mode of local transportation. Owning cars is forbidden in almost all Old Order Amish churches. Amish people are generally permitted to ride in cars driven by outsiders if they need to travel long distances.

In my years around the Amish, I've seen horse-drawn buggies of every imaginable shape, size, and color. To understand the Amish, one must appreciate the central role that the horse-drawn buggy plays in their life. The horse-drawn buggy is more than a mode of transportation, it's an important symbol of separation. Embracing the automobile would be, in the minds of most Amish, surrendering the simple way of life they have embraced.

The needs of the twenty-first century have forced the Amish to make use of the automobile much more than in previous generations. It is nearly impossible in today's society to, for instance, travel by buggy to attend a funeral hundreds of miles away. So for long distances and work-related trips, the church usually permits travel in an automobile.

Most large Amish communities, including the Eichers', have a craftsman that specializes in making buggies. The carriages can range from small two-seaters that aren't much more than a cart to sleek, plush behemoths that can comfortably carry a family of fourteen. The Eichers' buggy is very typical of most Amish ones, seating all ten family members quite comfortably. Buggies are made according to the dictates of the local church rules (ordnung). Some Amish sects are vehemently opposed to the orange "slow-moving vehicle" triangle required by some states. There have been court challenges by the ultraconservative Swartzentruber (see page 108) Amish church members. The Swartzentrubers prefer lining the back borders of their buggies with gray reflective tape. In Indiana, Amish buggy owners are required to display a license plate. The plate is similar to what is seen on cars, and the funds used for plate purchase are used for road repair, as the horse-drawn buggies can sometimes be tough on asphalt.

Covered buggies are the rule in most Amish settlements. There are a few, however, where a sheltered buggy is not permitted. These are the so-called "Swiss Amish" communities, whose inhabitants trace their lineage to Switzerland, not Germany, like the majority. These Amish speak a slightly different dialect than is commonly found elsewhere, and they continue different traditions, one of which is the open buggy. Open buggies are found primarily in Adams County, Indiana, and Webster County, Missouri. These buggies of course expose their occupants to the elements. However, the closed buggy is somewhat claustrophobic and rocks more during the wind and in the wake of passing trucks.

Most buggies are black and made of sturdy oak or hickory. There are exceptions, though. An Amish community in Mifflin County, Pennsylvania, uses yellow- and white-topped buggies. In addition to the Old Order Amish, Old Order Mennonites in Ontario, Canada, and Virginia, and some Old Order German Baptist Brethren near Delphi, Indiana, use buggies.

The more progressive the Amish community, the more amenities found on a buggy. Some buggies come with brakes, windshield wipers, a cup holder, and battery-powered lights. Some Amish settlements allow for rubber buggy wheels with plenty of tread, and on cold winter days, the buggy occupants can fire up a mini propane-operated heater. That is an improvement over the earlier generations of Amish, who kept warm in their buggies with blankets and covered pots of hot water.

One Amish man I met waved at his wipers dismissively.

"Why would I use those?" he asked me rhetorically as he pulled a bottle out of a small velvet bag. "I just use Rain-X."

TOMATOES

By mid- and late summer, our garden is usually full of ripe red tomatoes ready to be sliced onto sandwiches, made into sauces, diced into salads, and, perhaps our favorite use of all: homemade vegetable juice.

For tomatoes, I go to the local greenhouse and buy them as small plants, but you can start from seed. Mom used to do the seeds in what was called a "hot bed," which was just a mini outdoor greenhouse. She'd start them by a small window in the house right after the holidays, perhaps in late January or February.

For me, it is just better to go out and buy the plants; perhaps when the children are older I'll try from seeds. One of my favorite tomatoes is the Big Beef. I like anything with the name "beef" in it, because as the name says they are really "meaty" type tomatoes. They make good slicing tomatoes without many seeds. Early Girl is another tomato I often get because that one gives tomatoes earlier in the season, which I like. Romas are a good canning tomato, so I always get a few of those plants. Better Boys are a nice slicing tomato. Mom would always also grow nonacid tomatoes because Dad would eat those. I always plant a few of those. Little Lovina likes the orange color; she always says she wants the "orange tomatoes."

BAKED STUFFED TOMATOES

Serves 4

This is a great main dish during tomato season. For a heartier version, you can cook some ground beef and stuff it into the tomatoes with the rest of the mixture, but we think it tastes good just like this!

4 large tomatoes

Salt for sprinkling, plus ½ teaspoon

1 cup fresh bread crumbs

2 tablespoons butter, melted

1 egg, beaten

1 tablespoon minced onion

1 teaspoon minced fresh parsley

Few grains of ground pepper

Preheat the oven to 350°F. Grease a shallow baking dish.

Cut a slice from the top of each tomato. Scoop out the pulp with a spoon. Sprinkle the insides of the tomatoes with salt. Place the tomato shells in the prepared dish.

Put the bread crumbs in a small bowl and drizzle the melted butter over them; toss lightly to coat. Lightly mix in the egg, onion, parsley, the ½ teaspoon salt, and the pepper. Spoon the mixture into the tomato and bake until firm, about 30 minutes. Remove from the oven and serve hot.

TOMATO PANCAKES

Makes 2 dozen 4-inch pancakes

You wouldn't want to use maple syrup on these "pancakes"! This is a good way to get rid of some of those extra tomatoes during the height of the season. Like zucchini patties (page 64), this is a quick dish that goes over well around here with the children.

4 large eggs, lightly beaten
2 cups diced tomatoes with their juice
40 saltine crackers, crushed
Salt
2 tablespoons butter

Combine the eggs, tomatoes, crackers, and salt to taste in a bowl. Stir to blend, then shape the mixture into 4-inch pancakes.

Melt the butter in a large skillet over medium heat. Add the pancakes and fry for about 2 minutes on each side until lightly browned. Serve warm.

TOMATO GRAVY

Makes 5 cups

This is something my mother used to make a lot. It tastes great on pork chops, mashed potatoes, meat loaf, or a roast.

4 cups tomato juice
1 cup milk
2 tablespoons all-purpose flour
Salt and pepper to taste

Bring the tomato juice to a boil in a medium nonaluminum saucepan over high heat. Stir the milk and flour together in a small bowl and whisk it into the tomato juice. Bring the mixture to a boil while whisking constantly. Remove from the heat and serve.

These ultraversatile vegetables are the ultimate
signatures of summer in an Amish garden.
Tomatoes will quickly find their way into soups,
stews, and spreads as summer turns to fall.

Homemade Vegetable Juice

This is one of the favorite beverages in our house. A cold glass of spicy vegetable juice on a chilly winter morning is the thing to start the day, so we make a lot of it during the summer. I will put almost anything into homemade vegetable juice. My sister Emma and I joke about whether we are making V-6, V-7, V-8, or V-9 juice, depending on what we are putting in.

Making the juice is an all-day event. First, I round up as many of the children as I can and head out to the garden and fill bags with homegrown tomatoes. Up on our front porch we set up a table with a big bowl of water to soak the tomatoes in once we bring them up from the garden. Next to the bowl sits a large stainless-steel 20-quart cooker. If we do the juice on a Saturday when Joe is home he sure is a big help! He will slice out all the "bad" or bruised parts of the tomatoes, a long process that one has to be careful doing. Then after all the rotten parts are cut away, the tomatoes are cut in half and thrown into the cooker. Once the cooker is filled, then it is time to head into the kitchen.

We then add all the other vegetables that we might want in our juice. This could include carrots, celery, green beans, onions, and cucumbers. My sister Emma will really experiment with it. She'll put in potatoes, and even corn. Some people put red beets into their juice, but that is the one thing I won't put in. It just gives the whole juice a bright red color if they are added, which is not the most appetizing. Hot peppers are *always* added to give the drink an extra kick. Without the hot peppers, even just a few, it tastes dull. For the jalapenos, I take the stem off and just put them in whole. The jalapenos can get hot. I have rubber gloves so I don't worry much about it, but if you have a little baby you have to watch it because if you touch them before removing your gloves it will really burn after handling the peppers. The sting can also be bad if you rub your eyes, so we try to avoid doing that.

All the vegetables are cooked in the pot for about an hour. Someone will need to stir the cooker every few minutes to make sure that all the vegetables cook through.

After all the vegetables are cooked, we run them through

a "Victoria strainer," which is a hand-cranked juicer that separates the juice from the vegetable part. The juice goes into a bowl, and then we put it into sterilized jars. The jars are processed and then stored in the cellar to await a chilly winter morning. We like the juice best during the cold winter. It just makes it seem like summer when opening a jar and smelling the vegetables inside. But we enjoy homemade vegetable juice year-round.

Usually we will just drink a glass or two in the morning, but my brother-in-law Jacob can drink a whole quart of this on a Saturday morning. The homemade drink is packed with so many vegetables and vitamins I'm sure it would be difficult to drink too much of it!

HOMEMADE VEGETABLE JUICE

Makes 14 quarts

I tried to sit down and make a recipe and that is what I will share with you readers. But you can add whatever vegetables you want. I always put in more tomatoes than anything else. I like to add a lot of extra jalapenos as we like the spicy flavor they give. We love to drink this for breakfast on weekends. There is not a rule on how much of anything to put in.

15 pounds tomatoes, cut into chunks

4 onions, diced

4 green bell peppers, seeded and diced

6 large jalapenos, diced

6 small potatoes, peeled and diced

3 carrots, peeled and diced

3 stalks celery, chopped

3 cucumbers, sliced

2–3 teaspoons garlic powder

Salt

Combine all the ingredients except the salt in a 3-gallon stainless-steel pot over medium-high heat. Cook until soft enough to go through a Victoria strainer, about 30 minutes. Strain and put into sterilized quart jars and add 1 teaspoon salt to every jar. Drink the juice fresh, or see page 81 for information on home canning.

A NOTE ON HOME CANNING

Home canning is not an activity for the uninitiated. For Amish homemakers, home canning remains a vital part of feeding the family year-round. Often, techniques are passed down from mother to daughter through the generations.

Cleanliness is crucial when preparing canning jars. Lovina describes its importance like this: "Mom was always really picky about making sure there wasn't even a speck of dust in those jars. We use very hot water to clean our jars."

Lovina and many Amish homemakers use a method known as "cold packing" for canning. The term refers to packing food directly into storage jars raw and then processing in a boiling-water bath, making sure the jars are completely submerged in boiling water. The more accurate term for cold pack is "raw pack," but most Amish do not use the term. The USDA no longer considers the cold-pack method safe, but the practice is still widely used in Amish kitchens, including Lovina's, so that is why we're using it here.

To process foods using the cold packing method, fill sterilized jars with food, leaving about ¼ inch of headspace for jams, jellies, and juices, and about ½ inch of headspace for firmer foods like pickles, sauces, or relishes. Wipe any drips off of the rims of the jars. Attach the seals and lids.

Place the jars in a large pot and cover with water that is similar in temperature to the con-tents. Bring the water to a boil. The processing times will depend upon the contents (a reference to consult is homecanning.com). Carefully remove the jars from the boiling water and set them aside to cool gradually on a towel at room temperature. Store in a cool, dark place until ready to use.

Canning using a pressure cooker is today the USDA recommended method for home canning. Before practicing home canning, consult the USDA's updated rules on the Web or check with your local county extension agent.

A CULTURE OF CONTRADICTIONS?

The Amish are a closed culture that shuns all forms of technology. That's the popular, albeit untrue, perception of the Amish. So when people hear of an Amish person traveling in an automobile or using a telephone they often snicker at the seeming contradiction. But ask an Amish person if simply using a phone goes against his or her lifestyle and one receives a very different answer.

"It can really interfere with family life if it is in the house all the time," an Amish person remarked to me about the telephone.

The Amish draw a clear distinction between *using* and *owning* an item. For example, if Amish families were allowed to own automobiles, their close-knit communities would quickly collapse. Non-Amish America has become a disconnected, isolated suburbia. But simply riding in a car into town with a non-Amish neighbor to get some groceries is not viewed as wrong.

If it were up to most Amish, they'd still be a largely self-sufficient, isolated, agrarian community much as they were well into the twentieth century. But as farming gradually became a less viable way to make a living and with the outside world encroaching ever more, the Amish have struck a Faustian bargain with technology: Pick and choose wisely. A technology can be adopted in limited ways if it doesn't undermine the ultimate goal of creating a close-knit, self-sufficient existence. Of course, getting everyone to agree on what does and doesn't undermine that goal has created great debate and many splits within the Amish church. Some Amish sects remain totally opposed to even the most mundane technological advances, while other settlements have warily embraced cell phones and gasoline motors. So the contradictions some may see in an Amish person riding in a car or talking on a telephone are part of a very well-crafted bargain. While there are many sects of Amish (see page 108), there are even variations within the Old Order Amish, which is the church Lovina belongs to. Some Old Order Amish churches embrace technology more liberally, toting cell phones and riding gasoline-powered tractors. Others avoid almost all modern conveniences, including indoor plumbing.

The slow embrace of technology has come to Amish kitchens also. Some Amish communities, including Lovina's, now permit propane-powered refrigerators and freezers, a bow to proper food hygiene. But you won't be seeing George Foreman Grills or Magic Bullet blenders in Amish kitchens any time soon.

Lovina's church seems to be a very typical Old Order Amish church—that is, somewhere in the middle, not rejecting all new technologies nor or embracing them all either.

CARROTS

Carrots are harvested later in the summer. I like to plant them in rows. The carrot tops grow together, so you have one continuous row of tops to sort through. The problem is that the tops of garden-grown carrots are so thin that weeds get in there and they are difficult to hoe. The seeds are really tiny, like lettuce seeds, so you just put them in a row and let them go. My favorite varieties to plant are called Danvers and Tender Sweet. We just like the taste.

There aren't many vegetables that I buy in a store, and carrots are no exception. I usually like to grow my own carrots, and especially enjoy them in homemade vegetable juice. I think carrots are easy to grow. Mine don't get as big as they do in a store. They are big enough, but I don't have luck getting them really big. It seems like the carrots you grow at home get wider and fatter, whereas the carrots in the store are long sticks.

The wild rabbits like to clip the tops of the carrots in our garden, and when they do that the carrots will quit growing. Carrots are something the first frost won't hurt too badly since they are underground. Mom would cover them during the season's first frosts. and they'd survive just fine.

We always store our carrots in the basement after we pick them. They'll stay good in the basement for a long time. Leave a little of the top on. I remember one year I stored them in an old milk can and kept them covered and they did fine. Some years I'll just store them in something that isn't tight so they won't get mushy. A five-gallon bucket with the lid on loosely usually works well.

My children love carrot sticks, either just raw as a snack or in a dip. When my babies were teething I would give them a big carrot to chew on. I'd make sure it was a really long carrot so that they couldn't choke on it. It seemed to really make their gums feel good, and they could chew on it for a long, long time.

SUSAN'S CARROT BARS

Makes 20 bars

The children enjoy eating carrots just as a snack, but this is another way to get them to eat and enjoy them. You can use any kind of frosting that you like for these, but I like to use a cream cheese icing. My daughter Susan especially enjoys preparing these bars.

1 cup sugar

¾ cup vegetable oil

2 eggs, beaten

1 cup all-purpose flour

1 teaspoon baking soda

1 teaspoon ground cinnamon

½ teaspoon salt

1 cup shredded carrots

½ cup walnuts (optional)

Cream Cheese Frosting (page 87)

Preheat the oven to 350°F. Grease a 9 by 13-inch baking pan.

Stir the sugar, oil, and eggs together in a large bowl until blended. Combine the flour, baking soda, cinnamon, and salt in a medium bowl and stir with a whisk to blend. Add the dry ingredients to the wet ingredients and stir to blend. Add the carrots and nuts and stir until you have a smooth batter.

Pour the batter into the prepared pan and smooth the top. Bake until a toothpick inserted in the center of the cake comes out clean, 35 to 40 minutes. Frost.

CHEESY CARROT CASSEROLE
Serves 6 to 8

During "carrot season" we'll eat this as a main dish for supper. We eat meat with many of our suppers, but sometimes it is nice to have just vegetables for a change of pace. This colorful casserole is very filling for a meatless meal!

2 pounds carrots, peeled and cut into ½-inch slices
⅔ cup chopped onion
5½ tablespoons margarine or butter
2½ tablespoons all-purpose flour
¼ teaspoon salt
¼ teaspoon celery salt
¼ teaspoon dry mustard
⅛ teaspoon pepper
1¼ cups milk
5 ounces Velveeta cheese
2¾ cups cubed day-old bread

Preheat the oven to 350°F. Grease a 9 by 13-inch baking dish.

Put the carrots in a large kettle and cover with water. Bring to a boil, reduce the heat, cover, and simmer the carrots until tender, about 10 minutes. Drain and set aside.

Melt 2 tablespoons of the margarine in a large saucepan over medium heat. Add the onion and sauté until tender, about 5 minutes. Stir in the flour, salt, celery salt, mustard, and pepper. Gradually add the milk. Bring the mixture to a boil, then stir for 2 minutes. Add the cheese and stir until melted. Add the carrots and stir to coat.

Transfer the mixture to the prepared baking dish. Melt the remaining 3½ tablespoons margarine. Toss it with the bread cubes and sprinkle the bread over the carrots. Bake for 50 to 60 minutes, or until heated through.

CARROT CAKE

Serves 6

This sweet treat is probably a child's favorite way of all to eat carrots. Many adults like it, too—my sister Susan is also a fan of carrot cake.

2 cups sugar

1½ cups vegetable oil

4 large eggs, beaten

2 cups all-purpose flour

2 teaspoons baking soda

2 teaspoons ground cinnamon

1 teaspoon salt

3 cups peeled and grated carrots

⅓ cup chopped walnuts

1 cup raisins

CREAM CHEESE FROSTING

1 pound powdered sugar, sifted

1 (8-ounce) package cream cheese, softened

4 tablespoons margarine or butter, softened

1 teaspoon vanilla extract

½ cup chopped walnuts

Preheat the oven to 350°F. Grease a 9 by 13-inch cake pan.

Mix the sugar, oil, and eggs together in a large bowl. Combine the flour, baking soda, cinnamon, and salt in a medium bowl. Stir with a whisk to blend. Stir the dry ingredients into the wet ingredients. Add the carrots, nuts, and raisins and stir to blend. Pour the batter into the pan and smooth the top. Bake until a toothpick inserted in the center of the cake comes out clean, 35 to 40 minutes. Remove from the oven and let cool completely.

To make the frosting: Cream the sugar, cream cheese, and margarine together in a medium bowl. Stir in the vanilla and pecans. Spread on the cooled cake.

CORN

We can't wait for the summer corn crop to ripen each year so we can enjoy fresh buttered corn on the cob. There are so many ways to enjoy corn, and not all of them involve eating. There is a tradition (that seems to be disappearing with the older generation) of Amish using corn husks to fill their mattresses. They'd have to restuff them every year, and they'd even stuff pillows with the husks. My grandpa's mattress was like that. It would just sink down wherever you were on it. One time I stayed there overnight, and I thought the corn mattress was so uncomfortable. In the morning I woke up all scrunched in one area of the bed. To most younger people today, the cost of a mattress would be worth not having to stuff it once a year. And the corn mattresses were dusty. But back then they did not look at it that way.

I usually buy my corn seed by the cupful, and I think I put out about 2½ cups of seed. Usually, it is in the ground by mid-May, and then the juicy suppers of corn on the cob are just a few months away! When the corn is ready for harvest, starting in July, we enjoy eating it right off the cob. Or, almost right off the cob! We husk it and boil the ears for five minutes and then enjoy! I do like to grow enough, though, so I always have some left to can. That way we can have corn year-round. I like frozen corn, but I like my home-canned corn better; nothing can beat that. In addition to eating corn on the cob, Joe likes it fried. Frying corn is easy. All you do is take it off the cob and fry it in butter. Another way I use corn is in a homemade vegetable soup (see Grandma's Soup on page 99).

I like to grow Seneca sweet corn, Silver Queen, and Kandy Korn. I like to try different varieties and keep track of what we like the best. Mom would never plant anything but a type called NK. NK is a popular canning corn.

Another type of corn to grow is popcorn. Popcorn is something I haven't tried growing, but Mom did. The

homegrown popcorn was pretty good. The kernels are harder
and it isn't ready for harvest until later, toward the frost.

It takes a lot of time to can corn, more time than
it does for other vegetables. All that husking, removing
it from the cob, and putting it in the jars. It is a big job.
When I was living at home, we'd start in the morning and
husk until noon, and then Mom would take it all off the
cob, usually just scraping it off with a knife. It is a time-
consuming process. Some Amish communities used to hold
"corn-husking bees," where everyone would gather together
and just start husking corn. It'd be a day of food, fellowship,
and fun, and a lot of husking would get done. Seems it'd
be a fun way to get it all done, but that is also a tradition
that seems to be fading away. Perhaps they still do them in
other communities. Today, my younger children really enjoy
husking, but then you have to remove all the silk, which
isn't quite as easy to do.

CORN PUDDING

Serves 4 to 6

2 large eggs, separated
Kernels cut from 6 ears corn
¼ cup milk
½ teaspoon salt
⅛ teaspoon ground pepper

Preheat the oven to 350°F. Butter a 4-cup casserole.

In a large bowl, beat the egg yolks until they are thick and pale in color. Add the corn and mix thoroughly. Stir in the milk, salt, and pepper.

Beat the egg whites in a large bowl until soft peaks form. Carefully fold them into the corn mixture. Pour the mixture into the prepared casserole.

Prepare a hot-water bath: Bring 4 quarts of water to a boil. Set the casserole in a deep pan on the oven rack. Pour boiling water into the pan until it is level with the mixture in the casserole. Bake until firm, about 30 minutes.

CORN CASSEROLE
Serves 6 to 8

This is a good main dish during corn season; it makes a very hearty supper! To add extra color, you can add chopped red and green peppers.

1 pound bacon

½ cup (1 stick) margarine or butter

½ onion, chopped

½ cup chopped celery

5 tablespoons all-purpose flour

2 cups sour cream

Kernels cut from 6 ears corn

Salt and ground pepper

1 tablespoon minced fresh parsley

Preheat the oven to 350°F. Butter a 9 by 13-inch baking dish.

Cook the bacon in a large skillet until crisp. Transfer to paper towels to drain, then crumble and set aside. Melt the margarine in a large saucepan over medium heat. Sauté the onion and celery until soft. Stir in the flour, then the sour cream, until well combined. Add the corn and most of the bacon bits and season with salt and pepper to taste. Pour into the prepared dish and sprinkle on the remaining bacon bits and the parsley. Bake until lightly browned, 30 to 45 minutes.

AMISH TEX-MEX?

Jalapenos. Salsa. Tacos. These aren't the foods that typically come to mind when a person thinks of "Amish food." Amish cooking, however, is a bit like tofu: It absorbs the flavors of whatever is around it.

The Amish and their closely related Mennonite brethren have been journeying to Mexico for generations. Old Order Mennonites were lured to northern Mexico in large numbers during the 1920s. The government of Mexico, looking to revive a slumping agricultural economy in the north, promised the agrarian Mennonites that they could live without intrusion and free from compulsory military service. Canada, at the time, did not offer such assurances when it came to conscription, so Mexico had an appeal to the pacifist Mennonites. (The Amish are pacifists, too, and today, Amish and Mennonites in both the United States and Canada are permitted to claim "conscientious objector" status if faced with conscription.)

The Mennonites have isolated farming enclaves in rural Chihuahua state to this day. Intermarriage with native Mexicans is rare, so the communities are islands of German-speaking, blond-haired and blue-eyed peoples in this Hispanic country. Among the crops Mennonites in Mexico raise are jalapenos, tomatillos, and cilantro, which they sell at local produce markets and inevitably bring to their relatives back in Canada and the United States, spreading a love for traditional Hispanic flavors into other Anabaptist communities. (For more on Anabaptist sects, see page 108.) The Amish and Mennonites are prolific recipe- and seed-sharers, so a taste for Tex Mex spread among the Anabaptists.

Even without the Mennonites settling in Mexico, it was likely only a matter of time before the Amish "discovered" the culinary charms south of the border. Over the past twenty years, Old Order Amish have been traveling with increasing frequency to Mexico for medical treatment. Clinics catering to a largely Anabaptist clientele have sprung up in Tijuana, where the Amish seek out remedies not available in the United States, or, at the very least, less expensive medical care, since they don't carry traditional medical insurance.

And even if the Amish didn't go to Mexico for medical treatment they probably would still have be serving salsa, thanks to the growing presence of "Mexican" fast-food chains, supermarket salsas, and breakfast burritos across the United States.

Salsa is a natural dish for Amish homemakers to prepare. Tomatoes are a staple of Amish gardens, and salsa is a great way to use up those extra tomatoes. For centuries, Amish and Mennonite culinary culture has been "plain," so the spiciness of homegrown hot peppers probably has a lot of appeal. Other ethnic foods, such as Italian, Cajun, and Chinese, have not caught on as much among the Amish, although pizza enjoys popularity among the Anabaptists.

LOVINA'S HOMEMADE SALSA

Makes 14 quarts

The Clear Jel mentioned in the recipe sometimes generates reader mail when Lovina mentions the ingredient in her column. Clear Jel is a cornstarch-based thickener that is available at most grocery stores.

14 pounds tomatoes, blanched for 5 minutes,
   then peeled and chopped
5 cups chopped yellow onion
10 green bell peppers, seeded and chopped
4 medium to large jalapenos, chopped
1 cup distilled white or apple cider vinegar
½ cup packed brown sugar
¼ cup salt
1 teaspoon garlic powder
2 teaspoons dried oregano
1 tablespoon ground cumin
1 tablespoon chili powder
10 tablespoons instant Clear Jel
3 cups water

Combine all the ingredients except the Clear Jel and water in a 3-gallon stainless-steel stockpot. Bring to a boil over medium-high heat and cook, stirring occasionally, for 45 minutes.

Stir the Clear Jel and water together in a medium bowl until smooth. Stir it into the salsa, then pour the mixture into sterilized quart jars and seal.

If you want to can and store the salsa, see page 81 for more information on home canning.

JALAPENOS

Joe's family introduced ours to peppers. My mother may have experimented with some tiny chili peppers, but it wasn't until we met Joe's family that we really developed a liking for spicy foods. When they first tried to get me to try them I didn't want to. I remember having a sore throat and my mom told me to try some of those peppers "that'll burn your sore throat out." But I wasn't so sure. I took me a while until I finally got the nerve to try them. I wasn't one of those daring ones who tried them right away.

With most of our family really enjoying the hot taste, I now plant jalapenos, banana peppers, and habaneros. Although some are ready to harvest by late July, it isn't until August and September that I really have enough for our family.

We like to just dice them up and put them on top of our food or in our vegetable juice (page 80). But once our family took a liking to them, Mom would grow them and we would be dicing up peppers to put on lots of different foods.

BACON-WRAPPED JALAPENOS

Serves 4 to 6

This is sort of a different way to fix jalapenos. We enjoy this as a change of pace during the summer when Joe does a lot of our cooking on the outdoor grill.

¼ cup cream cheese, softened

½ cup (or more) shredded Cheddar cheese

8 jalapeno peppers, halved and seeded

8 slices bacon, cut in half crosswise

Preheat the oven to 400°F. Line a jelly-roll pan with aluminum foil.

Put the cream cheese and Cheddar cheese in a small resealable plastic bag. Seal the bag and knead until the cheeses are well combined. Cut off a bottom corner of the bag and use it to pipe a generous portion of the cheese mixture into each of the jalapeno halves.

Wrap a piece of bacon around each jalapeno half. (If you prefer to cook them on a grill, use a toothpick to hold the bacon in place.) Place the peppers on a rack in the jelly-roll pan, cheese side up. Bake for 20 minutes or until the bacon is crisp.

MY HOMEMADE HOT PEPPER BUTTER
Makes 7 pints

One of the dishes that we like to use jalapenos in is a spread that we call "hot pepper butter." I like to spread this on my meat sandwiches in the wintertime. This is also good on cheese sandwiches. And some even eat the spread just by itself as a sandwich. It gives just enough extra flavor. My sister Emma, who really enjoys extra flavor, adds even more peppers than this recipe calls for. So you can adjust the amount of jalapenos to fit your taste.

42 jalapenos , chopped
2 cups yellow mustard
4 cups distilled white vinegar
6 cups sugar
1 tablespoon salt
1 cup all-purpose flour
1½ cups water

Grind the peppers in a food processor. (I use a hand-cranked one.) Put the peppers in a 6- to 8-quart stainless-steel stockpot. Add the mustard, vinegar, sugar, and salt and bring to a boil over medium heat. Make a paste with the flour and water and stir it into the mixture. Cook for 5 minutes. Immediately pour into sterilized half-pint jars and attach the seals and lids. The heat will seal the jars.

Note: See page 81 for more information on home canning.

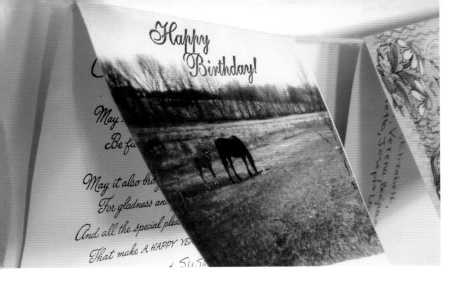

SUMMER OUTSIDE OF THE KITCHEN

Summer—July in particular—is full of birthdays (see page xix) in this household. In addition to birthdays, our wedding anniversary also falls in July. While we are celebrating the living, we take time out to pause and remember our dear mother who also had her birthday in the month of July.

My Mother: Elizabeth Coblentz (1936–2002)

Every July 18 I think of my dear mother. This special day marks her birthday.

I think I had the best mother anyone could have had. She was always concerned when we were sick and would doctor us back to good health. I remember her sitting up during the night to care for us doing all she could to keep us comfortable. She knew how to do reflexology on the feet and would often treat our feet. I miss her reflexology treatments, as they were relaxing. Often, while I was in labor with one of the children she would do the reflexology to help speed up the delivery. She was a comfort to have there when the six oldest children were born. She would prepare the meals for the children, Joe's aunt, the midwife, and anyone else who was there while I was delivering, and would hardly sit down, always finding something to clean while we waited for the new arrival.

We lived with my parents when our oldest child, Elizabeth, was born. She was a fussy baby during the night. Mom would come get Elizabeth and rock her and help get her quiet. She lost sleep to help me with the little one. When we children moved away from home she gave us boxes of groceries to help us start out on our own. She was kind and caring to everyone, and always had a friendly smile for all.

She would welcome friends to stay and eat with us, quickly preparing more food if they happened to drive in. She was a great cook and I still miss her cooking; my own cooking will never taste as good to me as hers did. Mom's food was always good; she just had a knack for making it tasty. She'd go by just feel, not a recipe. Her soups and stews were always seasoned just right. She was a great cook, but her food tastes were simple and she didn't waste anything. And out of all of her foods, there are two that really stand out: I never tasted potato salad as good as hers, and her pies.

I remember when I was first out of school and it was just Mom and me at home, she would slice a plate of tomatoes and green peppers and just have cold meat sandwiches for lunch. Sometimes she'd even just have tomato sandwiches. Her desserts were also always simple, too; she didn't make stuff that took a lot of extra ingredients.

Her care extended outside the kitchen. I remember when we were teenagers she would stay up in the rocker waiting for us to get home from being out with friends. When we were all back home, she could finally relax and go to sleep.

I remember her telling us to enjoy while we still have all the children living at home with us, when we could all fit in one buggy together. I could go on and on with the memories I have of my sweet mother. She is still close to my heart. When I was thirty-one and had six children and my baby only six weeks old, she passed away to a better land. Life goes on but we still think of her fondly, and she left behind a good example.

GROSZMUTTER

Lovina's note: It is sad that my youngest children will never have a memory of their grandmother, or *grozmutter*, which is the German word we use. I am grateful, though, that my oldest daughters have strong and special memories of her. I'm surprised how much Verena still remembers since she was only four when Mom passed away. Here is some of what they remember:

Elizabeth, age thirteen: The thing I remember most about my grandmother was the friendly smile on her face. She never would meet up with a person without a smile. And her cooking was delicious. I can still picture her standing by the kerosene stove with a long-handled spoon and stirring whatever was in the pot. My grandmother was always friendly and caring when I got hurt and loving when I was sad. When I left her house she would always give me a piece of candy. Sometimes she would say, "Don't let your Mom see

it, she might take it away." Then she would laugh when Mom would come around.

On our birthday, she would give each of us children a card with lots of candy and money in it. On our cards it would usually say the age of how old we were. I still have every single card she gave me. I remember when we lived in the trailer house on Grandma and Grandpa's farm. I would go over and knock on her door. I got all the attention I could want from her and from my aunts, Verena, Emma, and Susan. When my cousins came I did not like to share Grandma with them. My mom says I talked a lot at an early age, probably from being around so many adults every day.

We'd almost always be at Grandma's for Sunday supper. Most of the times all my cousins came, too. Grandma would fix a big meal to serve to her family. She never complained, although I think she was tired a lot. She said she was just glad her family came home to visit her. I was eight when my grandmother passed away. I remember sitting on the bench in front of her coffin as hundreds of people went through to see her for the last time. I remember as they lowered her coffin into the grave. I think that was the hardest part for everyone. I still remember where her grave is. She had lots of friends and people who met her who loved her. I know I do.

Susan, age eleven: I remember being at Grandma's house a lot. My mom and us children would spend one or two days a week at her house. Sometimes we'd stay there all night. I really liked that. We enjoyed jumping on the trampoline and liked to have water fights. Aunt Susan would always join us. Grandma made vegetable soup, which was our favorite. We called it "Grandma's soup." She would give us candy. Sometimes we would remind her before she went home if she didn't think about giving us some. I love my Grandma and miss her very much. I was six when she died and I felt sad. It wasn't until after Grandma and Grandpa's things were sold that I knew I would never see them again. But I hope I get to meet them someday in heaven.

Verena, age nine: I was four when my grandma died. But I can remember a lot about her. I remember the birthday and Christmas gifts. I like when all my uncles, aunts, and cousins had the Christmas gathering at my grandparents' house. They would give all of us children a gift that was wrapped up. It was exciting to open all our gifts. I remember Grandma coming to our house and sitting on a chair under our English walnut tree. She would crack the nuts open for us kids. We really liked them, and she had a hard time keeping up.

When we stayed at her house overnight, we'd treat her feet and brush her hair. She liked that. She gave us gum and candy. I miss her and still love her so much.

GRANDMA'S SOUP
Serves 6 to 8

We call this "Grandma's soup" because all my children remember this delicious homemade vegetable soup. They'll always think of their grandma when I make it for them. By the way, the recipe calls for one onion. I just put it in whole for flavoring and then remove it when the soup is done cooking. Mom would always eat the onion at the end, so that is a variation on the dish that you can try.

I use a pint of home-canned beef chunks instead of ground beef. The reason I like to use the beef chunks instead of ground beef is the broth from the beef chunks will give it a better flavoring.

1 pint of canned beef chunks
1 medium yellow onion
2 potatoes, peeled and diced
1 cup diced carrots
1 cup diced green beans
2 cups corn kernels
2 cups green peas
4 cups tomato juice
1½ teaspoons salt
1½ teaspoons ground pepper

Brown the beef chunks in a large skillet over medium heat. Put the beef chunks and the whole onion in a large pot and add the remaining ingredients. Add enough water to cover all the vegetables. Cook over medium heat until the vegetables are soft, about 30 minutes.

Summer Vacation

When the school closes its doors for the term, the children are always excited. And so am I, because I really welcome their help around the house during the months ahead. Running a household for ten people is a lot of work, and extra help is always welcome, plus it is just enjoyable to all be together.

With no homework to worry about, the children have extra time for fun during the summer. For instance, the boys like to go out in the lake with Joe to fish a lot. With them out in the boat, even though they wear lifejackets, I worry about them. So one summer I signed them all up for swimming lessons. They had fun and it makes me feel more safe. If they would fall in the water I couldn't get to them to save them, and Joe doesn't swim really well. It just seems we have more opportunities to go swimming here than in Indiana.

The girls have different things they like to do for fun. By the time Elizabeth hit her teen years she really liked to read books a lot. Some of the children's favorite authors are Janette Oke and Laura Ingalls Wilder. One summer, Susan and Verena read the whole *Little House on the Prairie* series. They took turns reading one paragraph at a time out loud. The other children would sit around and listen. I think this is a great way to learn, because if Verena pronounced a word wrong, Susan would step in to correct her.

Everyone learned that way. Elizabeth and Loretta also really enjoy being in the garden helping to weed and harvest.

On pleasant summer afternoons, a lot of times I make sandwiches and will pack up a picnic basket. The children like to sit outside on a blanket to eat their lunch. When they got older, Elizabeth and Susan sometimes didn't go out because they thought that the picnics were just something for the younger children. This gives me some peace and quiet and gives me a chance to get caught up on my work.

Another fun activity that all the children like to do outside is get together a game of kickball. Many summer afternoons are spent in the backyard, with makeshift bases and a ball for the games.

"Sleeping in" is also something the children enjoy during the summer. During the school year, they are up each day by 6 A.M. During the summer they usually sleep until 7 A.M., or if we are up later the night before they may even sleep later. I don't think they ever sleep past 8 A.M., though.

Summer schedules allow for a more relaxed breakfast also. When they are in school, I don't make such a big breakfast, just something easy like grilled cheese sandwiches or scrambled eggs. Pancakes are also quick and easy. During the summer, they really enjoy a homemade breakfast casserole, eggs and potatoes, or bacon. If I do make grilled cheese for them during the summer, I'll scramble some eggs to go with it.

**Summer Vacation "Pop Quiz Question":
What Is Your Favorite Part of Summer?**

Elizabeth: *Going barefoot, swimming, and biking*

Susan: *Being out of school, biking, and swimming*

Verena: *Swimming and biking*

Benjamin: *Pony-back riding, going fishing with
Dad in the boat, and not going to school and having
to do homework at night*

Loretta: *Pony rides, biking, catching lightning bugs,
and being out of school*

Joseph: *Riding my bike, playing in the sand, and going fishing*

Lovina: *Having picnics outside and having all of
my brothers and sisters home from school*

Kevin: *Having my brothers and sisters home from school*

Summer Chores

The children mostly get out of helping with the laundry when they are in school, because I'll do that in the mornings when they are gone. But during the summer when they are home, they help with it. Some of the children help wash, while others help to dry and fold. Usually, the girls have the chores in the house, while the boys do the outside ones. But if Joe has extra work outside, we'll usually send Loretta and Verena, although Susan is always quick to volunteer for outdoor work also.

Another chore that both boys and girls do is pulling weeds in the garden, although I really can't trust Benjamin and Loretta much yet. I made them weed the potatoes once and they were getting careless and started pulling the potatoes, not the weeds. It can be a little difficult to tell potatoes and weeds apart, so the younger ones will usually pull weeds around the corn. That is something they can weed easier because they can tell which are the weeds.

For outdoor chores, Benjamin and Joseph have to gather eggs, feed and water chickens, feed the horses, and give them hay. Kevin, even at barely two years old, is right there too following the older boys. That is how they learn. Joe is teaching Benjamin to feed the horses, but he overdoes it a bit. Sometimes Lovina—she's a little tomboy—goes along, too. Another outdoor chore is clearing stones. We have a lot of stones in the garden, and after Joe tills the boys will go behind and pick up stones.

While the boys do their chores, the girls are helping with dishes, sweeping the floors, ironing, baking, and mopping. It is surprising how young some of them are when they catch on and start helping with the chores. By age three or four, the children are really helping out, and my nine-year-old, Verena, is great at cleaning. It doesn't take long for her to get a room in order.

Each of the children has some chores that they'd rather do than others. For instance, Susan would rather be out in the barn taking care of the horses than washing dishes.

FISHING

My husband, Joe, likes to go fishing early in the morning or late at night. He usually heads to a nearby lake, which is just a few minutes away by buggy. Joe just hitches our little boat right up to the back of the buggy. Fishing is a fun activity for him that he has done most of his life. Joe always says that red worms and crickets are really good to catch bluegills, which are probably our favorite fish to eat. Other fish that Joe likes to catch include walleye, crappie, pike, and bass, but we don't like to eat those.

The most unusual thing he has ever caught was a snapping turtle. They cling to the mud, and he had to cut his line.

Salmon and perch are more up north, which his father has fished for before. But there really is nothing better-tasting as far as fish is concerned than a young bluegill. The fish is more tender tasting than any others we catch. At home, Joe's parents used to roll the fillets in eggs and flour and fry them. I usually deep-fry them in a batter or bake them. Either way, fresh fish is a tasty treat to have around here. We usually eat fresh fish most during the summer, because that is when Joe has the time to go fishing.

BAKED FISH

Serves 4 to 6, depending on size of fish

As I said, while Joe will sometimes catch catfish or crappies, our favorite fish to eat around here is bluegill. This is a pretty easy baked fish dish to prepare and I think it's healthier for the kids to eat than deep-fried, but we do like it that way also.

1 whole bluegill, 2 to 3 pounds, cleaned

5 cups water

Salt and ground pepper

6 saltine crackers, crushed

Dash of salt

1 tablespoon minced fresh parsley

1 tablespoon minced fresh thyme

1 tablespoon butter, melted

4 thin strips salt pork

2 cups cornmeal

Preheat the oven to 300°F. Butter a baking dish big enough to hold the fish.

Remove the head and tail of the fish. Put the head and tail a medium saucepan with the water. Simmer for 15 minutes to make a broth, adding salt and pepper to taste.

Combine the cracker crumbs, salt, parsley, thyme, and butter in a large bowl. Moisten the stuffing with 3 tablespoons of the fish broth. Stir to blend. Freeze the rest of the broth for another use. Stuff the fish with the stuffing and fasten with skewers.

Cut a few shallow slashes across both sides of the fish. Wrap the salt pork around the fish and roll it in the cornmeal. Bake until the flesh is opaque throughout, about 1 hour. Serve on a warmed platter.

Travel

We love seeing new places in the country and we have fun on the journey. It is exciting to see the children's eyes light up when they see something interesting or new. Of course, there is a lot of work in packing for a family of ten, especially for those not old enough to pack their own clothes. With the little ones, you need to take quite a few changes of clothes. Joe and I have always wanted to take a trip to the Great Smoky Mountains. We had planned to go right after our wedding, but then Joe's brother was hurt real badly and spent three months in the hospital. So we kept putting it off, but someday we hope to take our whole family there for a week. Amish are allowed to travel in cars, buses, and trains, but not in planes. There are, however, times when the church makes an allowance for planes, for example, when someone is sick.

The farthest we ever traveled together was to Kansas, which was a thirteen- or fourteen-hour drive. The next farthest was to Holmes County, Ohio.

When we traveled to Kansas, it took me a week to get all our clothes ready and packed. And then it probably took me a week to get everything washed and put away and back onto schedule again. Kevin was fourteen months and still taking a bottle, and it was endless what I needed for a three-day trip just for him. I have a habit of packing more clothes than we usually need. Next time, instead of packing everyone's clothes in separate suitcases, I would put a few clothes for everybody in one suitcase so we could just take in one every night.

Our children love to travel, but the younger children get fussy after riding too long. They like to pass time while driving by playing imaginative games like the license plate game, where they try to spot plates from as many different states as possible. Usually, one of the children will be in charge of keeping a list. They also like to play the alphabet game, where they try to be the first to spot letters on signs.

I enjoy traveling, as did my Dad. Mom was not a traveler; she preferred to stay close to home. Although I love to travel, I always look forward to coming back home; nothing is better than home sweet home.

PIZZA COOKIES

Makes 18 cookies

The children enjoy having snacks such as cookies, crackers, and popcorn while traveling. It was really a treat when we stopped at a Dairy Queen on the way back from Ohio and got them all a milkshake. Pizza cookies are a colorful cookie that is fun for kids to eat in the car. They are less messy than other cookies because they do not crumble as easily. A round pizza pan can be used for this, or a baking sheet.

½ cup granulated sugar

⅓ cup packed brown sugar

4 tablespoons (½ stick) margarine or butter

1 large egg

½ cup smooth peanut butter

1 teaspoon vanilla extract

1½ cups all-purpose flour

1 cup chocolate chips

2 cups mini-marshmallows

2 cups mini M&M's

Preheat the oven to 375°F.

Combine the sugars, margarine, egg, peanut butter, and vanilla in a medium bowl. Add the flour and mix until well blended. Press or roll the dough onto a 15-inch pizza pan or a baking sheet. Roll the dough to the edge of pan. Bake for 10 minutes. Remove from the oven and top with the chocolate chips, marshmallows, and M&M's. Return to the oven until the chips, marshmallows, and M&M's melt, 5 to 8 minutes. Remove from the oven and let cool completely. Cut into wedges or squares.

ANABAPTIST SECTS

The Amish are part of a much larger Protestant religious movement called the Anabaptists. The term *Anabaptist* is used to describe a sixteenth-century theology whose adherents reject infant baptism, believing that baptism should be bestowed only on adults. The Anabaptist movement includes several subgroups, including the Amish, Mennonites, Hutterites, and Pietism-influenced German Baptists.

The lack of a centralized structural government in the Amish church has resulted in numerous splits, both major and minor. Some of the more prominent subgroups of Amish and their identifying traits include:

OLD ORDER AMISH: In the "Old Order" Anabaptist movement, the ownership of automobiles is prohibited, and church members practice shunning, or expelling people from the church for committing acts that go against the church's beliefs. Church members are not permitted to have electricity or telephones in the home. Worship is held in homes.

NEW ORDER AMISH: This group split from the main Old Order Amish church in the 1960s. Church members still dress plainly, but allow telephones and electricity in their homes.

BEACHY AMISH: A small group of Amish, similar to New Order Amish, who allow automobiles and electricity, but still dress plainly and may attend church in a formal church building.

AMISH MENNONITES: A loose confederation of churches that have split from the Amish church but haven't quite joined the mainline Mennonite movement.

SWARTZENTRUBER AMISH: A small, ultraconservative sect of Amish found in Ohio. Group rejects most modern conveniences, including indoor plumbing and riding in cars, even if driven by non-Amish.

NEBRASKA AMISH: Widely considered the most conservative of all Amish churches. Named for an early bishop who spent time in Nebraska trying to develop an Amish colony, Nebraska Amish are found in small enclaves in Pennsylvania and Ohio.

OLD ORDER MENNONITES: Worship is held in formal church buildings. Members dress plainly and some travel by horse-drawn buggy.

MENNONITE CHURCH USA: The mainline Mennonite church. They embrace pacifist principles and adult baptism, but allow all forms of modern technology. They do not wear plain dress.

OLD GERMAN BAPTISTS: This group wears plain dress and is found in Ohio, Indiana, Kansas, and California. Worship is held in meetinghouses. Men greet with the "kiss of peace," a gentle touching of lips, on Sunday. Church members are allowed automobiles and electricity, but most don't own televisions or radios.

HUTTERITES: Very much like Old Order Amish in dress and theology, this group's lifestyle is communal. They are found mainly in Montana, Manitoba, Minnesota, and the Dakotas.

The days slowly grow shorter again and the first yellow
school buses begin to rumble down the roads by our house.
These are signals that summer is coming to an end.
A sense of urgency begins, as there is still much to do
before winter sets in. That is what fall is for.

autumn

Do not be proud and overbearing because you have been blessed with this world's goods . . . for God who has given can also take away, and may do so, if you through pride or contempt of others make misuse of His gifts to you.

—Excerpt from an Amish prayer

While autumn brings with it a beauty of turning leaves and bright orange pumpkins in the garden, it is also a time of much work to be done.

Canning, harvesting, and tilling the garden all need to be done before the first snows. Winter will soon arrive, and we must make sure we are prepared for whatever Mother Nature is going to send our way.

Homemade grape pie, freshly pressed apple cider, and crisp green peppers from the garden all add to the feel of fall. These foods are treats that we look forward to all year, especially that delicious homemade grape juice. The local apple orchards are full of fresh fruit that we eagerly pick. And fall also brings with it the chance for us to can chicken broth, which we'll use in soups during the cooler months ahead.

When I think of autumn arriving, I imagine all the leaves that need raking. We have a lot of trees in our yard, so there are plenty of leaves to get rid of this time of year. I also think of emptying out the garden and getting it all tilled for winter. Although I am glad to have a garden I am always relieved once it is cleared up and done for the winter. I am always thankful for all the canning of vegetables that I process each year. We are truly blessed.

Perhaps the biggest change that occurs in the Eicher household each fall is the arrival of a new school term. With autumn comes an end to the slow mornings of summer. It's back to school and back to the morning rush.

I get up to help Joe get ready for work around 3:15 A.M. Then sometimes I go back to sleep, or sometimes I'll just stay awake and catch up on things. If I do go back to sleep, I might sleep till quarter of six when the children have to get up.

I wake up the schoolkids around 6 A.M. and they head out for school around 7. Sometimes I wake them up a little earlier. But especially in the beginning of the school year they need all the sleep they can get. If a child didn't finish his homework the night before, I might have to get him up earlier. My girls have no problems with doing their homework, but Benjamin just hates doing homework.

I usually help the youngest ones get ready for school first. Each child has always been very excited to go for the first time. Joseph was a really good one; he was so eager to go. Elizabeth, Loretta, Verena, and Susan usually get all their clothes together themselves. The boys don't know where anything is so I have to help them. There is such a difference from one boy to the next. While one likes to be as neat as possible, the other doesn't care what he wears. I can see this changing though as they get older.

AMISH EDUCATION

Historically, the Amish have gone to public schools. Since the 1972 landmark U.S. Supreme Court Case *Yoder vs. Wisconsin*, a ruling that allowed the Amish to educate their children "as they see fit," the trend has slowly been shifting toward Amish parochial schools (the "one-room school"). The Supreme Court ruling allows the Amish to send their children to school just through the eighth grade regardless of whether they attend public or private school. The Eicher children attend public schools, which is fairly common for the Amish in their area.

One of their favorite breakfasts is pancakes. I usually make buttermilk pancakes. Sometimes I buy a box of cereal for a really quick breakfast. For a change of pace for breakfast, the kids sometimes like omelettes. When I fry eggs for everyone it can take about sixteen eggs and for scrambled eggs about two dozen. When our chickens were giving us five or six dozen eggs a day, we stayed away from anything with eggs. We got tired of them.

Most of the time, the children eat the lunch served at school. They like to pack their lunch once in a while. If they do want a packed lunch, we have to get up about a half hour earlier or do it the night before. Favorite packed lunch items include a ham sandwich, and maybe cookies and juice.

Packing lunches is part of my morning routine year-round because I always have to pack Joe's lunch. If he packed it himself he wouldn't put much in it, so I like to make sure he has a well-balanced meal. If it were up to him he'd just eat a tomato sandwich, but I think he needs meat. So I'll pack him a ham sandwich, and cookies or fruit—peaches and apples are favorites; he doesn't care for bananas much. Joe doesn't want as much in his lunch as a lot of his fellow factory workers. Since he doesn't eat as much I always make sure he has a half-gallon jug of ice water. Joe doesn't like to eat much while he is working. He'll just eat a little something from his lunch bucket and eat the rest on the way home from work, around 2 P.M. All in all, the days are more rushed once autumn gets here. But for my daughter Verena, fall is her favorite season.

WHY I LIKE AUTUMN
by Verena, age nine

My favorite season is fall. I like when the leaves fall off the trees. We rake the leaves in a big pile. Then we take turns hiding in them. We like to jump in them when we have a big pile. When someone comes, we hide in the pile and then we pop up and scare them. Our dog, Frisco, likes to lie in our pile of leaves, too. I like fall too because it is not so hot outside.

I like Thanksgiving and turkey. And I like when we don't have to mow the grass. I think fall is fun.

AUTUMN GARDEN GOODIES

Some fall-garden fruits and vegetables are ones we look forward to all year. Those big, beautiful orange pumpkins make their appearance in the autumn. Green peppers are really good and firm right up until that first frost. It's also a time of year we enjoy grapes, and, oh, how we love those crisp, fresh, juicy apples at the local orchards!

GREEN PEPPERS

I usually buy my green pepper plants from a local greenhouse when they are small seedlings. Some years, I have a lot come up in the garden. One year, when I thought we were going to get our first frost of the season, I went out in the garden and picked all the remaining green peppers. I collected enough to fill two large grocery sacks with them. Then the next morning, I awoke to find that it was only 47 degrees out. So I had all these picked peppers to figure out how to use!

In addition to the pepper plants I buy, they sometimes also just come up on their own in my garden from the leftover "kitchen slop" that is thrown into the soil as fertilizer. Sometimes there are seeds in the slop. I'll have watermelon, tomatoes, and green pepper plants all coming up in a tangle in the same spot from those seeds. I furnished a lot of Emma's tomato plants that way one year.

I usually plant several varieties of green peppers. I like to try different ones. One of my favorites, though, is California Wonder. I always have to have that variety. We just like the taste. We use a lot of chopped green peppers, mainly in tacos, sandwich spread, casseroles, and a popular meal that we call a "haystack supper." For those unfamiliar, a "haystack" is a layered meal of hamburger, lettuce, tomatoes, green peppers, and onions, sort of like a taco without the taco! Stuffing them is another good way to use green peppers.

I try to harvest the peppers while they are still green. I don't like the taste of them when they turn red. I just think they have a different taste after they turn, although Mom would eat them red and enjoy them.

STUFFED GREEN PEPPERS

Serves 4

A neighbor-lady told me that you can hollow out the green peppers ahead of time, stuff them with waxed paper, and freeze them, and they'll keep for a long time. Ever since she gave me that advice I have done mine that way and it really does work well. This recipe makes a very good supper!

1½ teaspoons salt

4 large green bell peppers

1 pound ground beef

1 tablespoon minced fresh parsley

½ teaspoon ground pepper

⅔ cup cooked rice

1½ cups canned tomatoes, pushed through a sieve

¼ cup finely chopped white onion

¼ cup water

4 slices mozzarella cheese

Preheat the oven to 350°F. Grease an 8-cup baking dish.

Fill a large pot with water, add ½ teaspoon of the salt, and bring to a boil over medium-high heat. Cut out the stems of the peppers and rinse out the seeds, leaving the peppers whole. Put the peppers in the boiling water, cover the pot, and cook for 5 minutes. Drain the pot and set the peppers aside to cool.

Brown the ground beef in a large skillet over medium heat. Drain off any excess grease. Stir in the remaining 1 teaspoon of salt, parsley, ¼ teaspoon of the ground pepper, and rice. Lightly fill the peppers with the mixture, heaping slightly. Stand the peppers upright in the prepared dish.

Combine the tomatoes, onion, water, and the remaining ¼ teaspoon of the ground pepper in a small bowl. Mix well. Pour over the peppers. Place a slice of cheese on each pepper. Bake until peppers are tender, about 25 minutes.

PIZZA CASSEROLE
Serves 4 to 6

This is typical of the type of casserole that we use green peppers in. Just chop them up and add them to it. For this recipe, I sometimes add a layer of pepperoni slices just before the cheese. This tastes like pizza, except without a crust. This is something that we'll prepare for the evening meal on the day we have church. It's an easy casserole to prepare more if additional guests arrive.

1 pound ground beef

⅓ cup chopped onion

½ cup diced green bell peppers

1 (4-ounce) can sliced mushrooms, or 4 ounces of fresh sliced mushrooms

½ teaspoon salt

8 ounces spaghetti, cooked

2 (10-ounce) cans pizza sauce

2 cups shredded mozzarella cheese

Preheat the oven to 350°F. Grease a 9 by 13-inch baking dish.

Brown the ground beef with the onion and green pepper in a large skillet over medium heat. Drain the grease. Stir in the mushrooms, salt, and cooked spaghetti, and spoon the mixture into the baking dish. Pour the sauce over the top and sprinkle with a layer of cheese. Bake until the cheese has melted and the casserole is bubbling, about 30 minutes.

GRAPES

Grapes are ready to be picked in the fall, and Concord grapes have become one of our favorite fall foods. In the vineyards around here, some grapes are bigger, some are smaller, but most are bigger than a marble. The color of homegrown grapes is a little different from what you might see in the supermarket—these are a cloudy purple, and they have seeds. These grapes are best for canning, not snacking. Some of my kids were getting stomachaches from eating the Concord grapes and swallowing the seeds, so I buy store-bought seedless for snacks.

Some Amish have grapes in their gardens, others do not. Those who don't have their own grapes go to a local Amish-owned vineyard to pick some. One year nine different families (ours included) went at once to pick grapes.

The vineyard at this farm was amazing, with grapes all over the place. I couldn't believe how thick the grapes were. We brought along a twenty-foot enclosed trailer to store our harvest, and we had it all filled up. We picked for about ninety minutes. We had everything filled, sacks on top of one another. We brought home five bushels of grapes, green and purple. We all used five-gallon buckets to go along the rows of vines as we picked. We had storage bins that we'd pour the grapes into from our buckets. The men seemed to be able to pick quicker. I used scissors to cut the grapes off the vines, but some of the men used their thumbnails and just broke them off. It took a little more time using scissors.

My mother tried a few different times to grow grapes but it seemed like something was always getting into them—she never knew whether it was raccoons or rabbits. So finally she just stopped trying to grow them. I'd like to get some vines started and try growing them and just gradually add a few more.

We use the grapes for homemade juice and homemade grape jelly. I always liked grape jelly. Mom used to make the best batches!

There are several ways you can make homemade grape juice. A lot of the women out here put their grapes in a steamer and when they are steaming the juice will fall to the bottom. They add sugar and make a concentrate to just add water to later. But I'd rather have mine ready to drink as soon as the jars are opened. I think that when the water is cooked right in with the grapes instead of adding water later the flavor is better. I think a concentrate tastes too much like those frozen juices. I used to do what Mom did and put grapes right into the can and put sugar and water in and cold pack it. Then you'd just have to strain it when you opened it. Every time I'd open a can of grape juice, I'd use a strainer. But now I prepare it so it can be poured into jars and be ready to drink!

Making homemade grape juice takes a lot of sugar. When I made grape juice using 2½ bushels, I used 35 pounds of sugar to make 150 quarts of juice. Some years, I cut down on my sugar, say a cup of grapes to a cup of sugar. I don't like sour grape juice,

but I don't like it too sweet either. The kids get enough sugar other times in other foods, so I like to keep the juice with just a hint of sweetness.

Home processing grape juice is a messy job. First we stem and wash the grapes, usually the evening before making the juice. It is a family effort, with Joe and the children stemming and me washing. I'll whip up a supper of eggs, potatoes, and bacon as a reward for helping me. Joe likes that because he's often too rushed in the mornings to have a good breakfast, so breakfast for supper is a treat. Processing grapes is something the whole family can do, but one year, when they were younger, I made Lovina and Joseph quit because they wanted to squeeze the juice out of the grapes before they were washed.

I love the smell when you are making grape juice; it is a flavorful smell, not like when you can meat or vegetables. It has a sweet fragrance to it.

HOMEMADE GRAPE JUICE
Makes 4 to 6 quarts

Our children love the green (Lovina calls them white) or purple store-bought grapes. But they won't drink store-bought grape juice. We all think it is too sweet. Some of the Amish process their juice for 10 to 15 minutes in boiling water and you can do that if you think you're going to keep home-canned grape juice for a long time. But around here it never lasts that long so I usually don't.

8 to 10 cups water
5 heaping cups Concord grapes
2½ cups sugar

Boil the water and grapes in a large pot for 45 minutes. Put the contents of the pot through a strainer or juicer. Put the juice back on the stove and add the sugar. Let the juice come to a boil, stirring to dissolve the sugar. Immediately pour into sterilized jars and attach the seals and lids. The heat will seal the jars.

Note: See page 81 for more information on home canning.

GRAPE SALAD

Serves 6 to 8

This is a good, light salad that is commonly served at the after-church supper in the evening. Other fruits can be added to this, like pineapple.

1 cup sour cream

8 ounces cream cheese, softened

1 cup sweetened whipped cream or whipped topping

1½ cups powdered sugar, sifted

1 teaspoon fresh lemon juice

3 pounds seedless grapes

Combine all the ingredients in a large bowl and stir until the grapes are coated evenly. Cover and refrigerate overnight before serving.

GRAPES AND PINEAPPLE IN SOUR CREAM

Serves 4

Here is another salad that is a favorite to serve on Sunday evening after church. This is a good colorful salad because of the pineapple.

2 cups seedless green grapes

1 (13-ounce) can pineapple chunks, drained

4 tablespoons packed brown sugar

⅓ cup sour cream

Combine the grapes and pineapple in a serving bowl. In a small bowl, stir 3 tablespoons of the brown sugar into the sour cream. Add to the fruit and toss to combine. Cover and refrigerate for at least 2 hours or overnight. Just before serving, sprinkle the salad with the remaining 1 tablespoon brown sugar.

CONCORD GRAPE STREUSEL PIE

Serves 4 to 6

This is a great pie to use with the juice grapes we pick at the vineyard. The children tried to eat the grapes just as a snack by themselves, but didn't care for the taste. In a pie, however, the Concord grapes have a different, better taste. I will share my homemade pie dough recipe, which you can use to prepare this pie and others in this book. The recipe is the same one my mother used for her pies, which I always thought were the best! The pie dough recipe makes three single 9-inch crusts.

FILLING

4½ cups Concord grapes

1 cup sugar

¼ cup all-purpose flour

2 teaspoons fresh lemon juice

⅛ teaspoon salt

STREUSEL

½ cup old-fashioned rolled oats

4 cup packed brown sugar

¼ cup all-purpose flour

4 tablespoons butter, softened

Preheat the oven to 425°F.

To make the filling: Seed the grapes, place them in a large saucepan, and cook over medium-high heat until soft, about 5 minutes. Drain off the liquid. Stir in the sugar, flour, lemon juice, and salt. Spoon the filling into the crust.

To make the streusel: Combine all the streusel ingredients in a medium bowl. Mix with your fingertips until it forms coarse crumbs. Sprinkle evenly on top of pie filling. Bake until golden brown, 35 to 40 minutes.

My Homemade Pie Dough

3 cups all-purpose flour

1 teaspoon salt

1 cup lard

1 large egg

⅓ cup cold water

1 tablespoon apple cider vinegar

To make the dough: In a large bowl, combine the flour and salt. Stir to blend. Add the lard and rub it into the flour with your fingertips until the mixture resembles coarse crumbs. Add the egg, water, and vinegar and stir with a fork until the dry ingredients are moistened. Form the dough into a ball and divide that into 3 balls. Form a ball into a disk and roll it out to a ⅛-inch thickness on a floured surface.

Fit the dough into a 9-inch pie pan and trim the edges to a 1-inch overhang. Fold the dough under and crimp the edges. If not using now, form the remaining 2 balls of dough into disks, place each in a resealable plastic bag, and freeze for up to 3 months.

PUMPKINS

By late September, large orange pumpkins begin to show themselves in area gardens. They are the whales of the garden! I love to grow my own pumpkins, but sometimes I can't because they take up so much room in the garden.

Mom always grew pumpkins and then canned the puree for pie filling. You can get a lot of pie filling out of a few pumpkins. Most years, Mom put a few plants out, but not every year, again because of space. As she began to go to the grocery store more, canned pumpkin pie filling got so cheap it wasn't worth her time to can it at home.

You have to be careful how and where you plant your pumpkins in the garden even if you do have the space, because of cross-pollination. (One year I put my watermelons next to my cucumbers, and the cucumbers ended up being round!) As much room as pumpkins take up, watermelons take up even more.

To can pumpkin, you chunk it up and cook it down, then put it through a sieve. Our strainer has a special "pumpkin screen" that filters the pumpkin pulp so we can use it for pies and cookies. I think homemade canned pumpkin resembles applesauce in color, but it is thicker than applesauce. Home-canned pumpkin puree, of course, needs to be seasoned for a pie. Store-bought pumpkin pie filling is seasoned already.

PUMPKIN PIE

Serves 6

Pumpkin pie was something Mom always fixed around Thanksgiving or whenever the big orange fruits were ready to harvest and begin canning.

1 disk My Homemade Pie Dough (page 125)

4 large eggs, separated

2 cups homemade pumpkin puree, or 1 (15-ounce) can pumpkin puree

½ teaspoon pumpkin pie spice

1 teaspoon vanilla extract

1 cup sugar

Pinch of salt

2 tablespoons all-purpose flour

2 cups milk, scalded

Preheat the oven to 400°F.

Roll the disk of dough out to a ⅛-inch thickness on a floured surface. Fit the dough into a 9-inch pie pan. Trim the overhang to 1 inch. Fold the dough under and crimp the edges.

Beat the egg whites in a large bowl until stiff, glossy peaks form. Beat the egg yolks in a small bowl.

In a large bowl, mix the pumpkin puree, egg yolks, pumpkin pie spice, vanilla, sugar, salt, flour, and milk together until the mixture is smooth. Fold in the egg whites. Pour the filling into the piecrust. Bake for 10 minutes. Reduce the oven temperature to 350°F and bake until the pie is set, about 40 minutes. Remove from the oven and let cool completely.

As the first frosts approach and autumn's first chills shiver through the air, the ovens begin to fire up offering a bounty of baked goods.

PUMPKIN BREAD
Makes 2 loaves

Pumpkin, like watermelon and squash, is a vine that really spreads out. So whether we grow pumpkins in a particular year depends largely on how much space we have. I like having fresh pumpkin because it really can be used in a lot of different baked goods. This moist bread is a seasonal favorite!

3½ cups all-purpose flour

3 cups sugar

2 teaspoons baking soda

1½ teaspoons salt

1 teaspoon ground cinnamon

2 cups homemade pumpkin puree, or 1 (15-ounce) can pumpkin puree

4 large eggs, beaten

⅔ cup water

⅓ cup vegetable oil

1 cup pecans, chopped

Preheat the oven to 350°F. Grease and flour two 9 by 13-inch loaf pans. Knock out the excess flour.

Combine the flour, sugar, baking soda, salt, and cinnamon in a large bowl. Stir with a whisk to blend. Stir in the pumpkin, eggs, water, oil, and pecans. Divide the batter evenly between the prepared pans. Bake until a toothpick inserted in the center of a loaf comes out clean, about 1 hour.

PUMPKIN COOKIES

Makes 2 dozen cookies

Pumpkin cookies are a favorite dessert to prepare for the gathering after church. They look almost like a sugar cookie but are the brownish color of pumpkin. This is a soft cookie that tastes very good with icing. The kids really like them.

1 cup vegetable shortening

2 cups sugar

4 cups all-purpose flour

2 teaspoons baking soda

2 teaspoons baking powder

2 teaspoons ground cinnamon

½ teaspoon salt

2 cups homemade pumpkin puree, or 1
    (15-ounce) can pumpkin puree

1 cup chocolate chips

ICING

½ cup milk

2 tablespoons butter

½ cup packed brown sugar

¾ teaspoon vanilla extract

½ cup powdered sugar

Preheat the oven to 350°F. Grease 2 baking sheets.

Combine the shortening and sugar in a large bowl and stir until smooth. Combine the flour, baking soda, baking powder, cinnamon, and salt in a medium bowl. Stir with a whisk to blend. Stir the dry ingredients into the wet ingredients, then stir in the pumpkin until smooth. Stir in the chocolate chips. Drop by teaspoonfuls 2 inches apart on the prepared pans. Bake until cookies become firm and edges begin to brown, about 8 to 10 minutes. Remove from the oven and let cool on the pans for 5 minutes. Transfer the cookies to wire racks to cool completely.

To make the icing: Combine the milk, butter, brown sugar, and vanilla in a small saucepan. Stir over low heat until the sugar is dissolved and the butter melted. Remove from the heat and let cool completely. Stir in the powdered sugar. Spread the icing on the cookies and let stand until the icing is set.

APPLES

Of course, fall is the time when apples are ready to harvest. One of my fondest memories of apple season is the time spent at my Uncle Chris's making apple butter.

We'd go to his house the night before, and we would sit around a table and peel apples all evening. The next morning, we would go back early and Uncle Chris would start the fire under the big black kettle so we could cook the apples down to make apple butter. Then they would divide it up evenly and we'd bring some home and put it in jars. The butter was almost like applesauce but a touch more sour. It was good. Mom would always have fresh or home-canned apple butter on the table year-round.

We would come home from school and there would be a dish of apple butter with warm homemade bread waiting for us. We would make apple butter sandwiches for ourselves as an after-school snack.

We had several apple trees at Mom and Dad's place. Every fall, we would have enough apples to make and can a lot of applesauce. Mom always enjoyed making the fall treat. My kids are just getting to the point where they like applesauce. They like to crumble a cookie into applesauce and eat it that way.

We don't have apple trees here at our home in Michigan. Joe doesn't like to prune apple trees. It is a lot easier to go out and buy bushels of apples and cider from an Amish farm down the road than to make those things ourselves.

APPLE CRISP

Serves 4 to 6

I fix this a lot. It looks a little like pie, but there's no dough. We like to eat it with a scoop of ice cream when it's warm. For this recipe, you can really use any apple, but I like to use Golden Delicious apples. Honey Crisp is another good cooking apple that goes well in this recipe.

5 large apples, peeled, cored, and thinly sliced (6 cups)
1 cup granulated sugar

TOPPING
1 cup (2 sticks) butter, slightly softened
1½ teaspoons ground cinnamon
1½ cups old-fashioned rolled oats
1 cup packed brown sugar
1 cup all-purpose flour

Preheat the oven to 350°F. Lightly grease a 9 by 13-inch pan.

Put the apple slices in the pan and sprinkle with the granulated sugar. Gently toss with your fingers to mix.

To make the topping: Combine the butter, cinnamon, oats, brown sugar, and flour in a medium bowl and mix with your fingertips until the mixture is coarse and crumbly. Spoon evenly over the apples. Bake until golden brown, about 45 minutes.

APPLE BARS

Makes 25 to 30 bars

My sister Susan likes to make apple bars. These are almost like brownies and are always a hit. You can see the little apple pieces on the top, and they taste really good warm.

3 large eggs

1 cup vegetable oil

1¾ cups sugar

2 cups all-purpose flour

1 teaspoon baking soda

½ teaspoon salt

½ teaspoon ground cinnamon

2 cups peeled, cored, and chopped apples

1 cup walnuts, chopped

Preheat the oven to 350°F. Grease a 9 by 13-inch baking pan.

Beat the eggs, oil, and sugar together in a large bowl. In a medium bowl combine the flour, baking soda, salt, and cinnamon. Stir with a whisk to blend. Stir the dry ingredients into the wet ingredients until blended. Stir in the apples and walnuts. Pour into the prepared pan and smooth the top. Bake until firmly set, like a brownie, 35 to 40 minutes. Remove from the oven and let cool. Cut into bars.

APPLE FRITTERS

Makes 10 to 12 fritters

Fritters are a bit like doughnuts, and are a favorite around here in the fall. We usually eat them for breakfast.

1 cup all-purpose flour
2 teaspoons baking powder
2 tablespoons sugar
¼ teaspoon salt
1 large egg, beaten
¼ cup milk
3 apples, peeled, cored, and chopped
Vegetable oil for deep-frying

Combine the flour, baking powder, sugar, and salt in a large bowl. Stir with a whisk to blend. Make a hole in the mixture and stir in the egg, milk, and apples.

Fill a deep-fryer or Dutch oven half full of oil and heat to 375°F. Drop batter by the tablespoonful into hot oil and fry until golden brown, just a few seconds on each side. Using a slotted spoon, transfer to paper towels to drain.

CHURCH: FOOD AND FAITH

There are many aspects to our church life that are celebrated with food. And food is also used to help those in need. Whether it be a "grocery shower" for a shut-in or a new mother, or offering food for donation to help raise money for medical bills, food plays an important part in our faith.

Food Drives

One enjoyable thing about our church is that everyone tries to help one another out if someone experiences a problem. If a family has medical bills that are just too high to pay, people pitch in to help. One way to raise money for hospital costs is through a food drive. I've participated in a pizza drive, and some in my family have participated in a submarine sandwich drive. There are also doughnut drives. The goal is to prepare as much food as possible to sell to people in our community, and the proceeds will be used for medical bills.

For the pizza drive, the ingredients were purchased from an Amish-owned bulk food supplier. The crusts were already prepared; women from our church just had to assemble the pizzas. We all gathered at the home of one of our church members. The assembly lines began at 3:30 P.M., and the next five to six hours were spent putting together over three thousand pizzas. There were four different lines: one for meat lovers; one for mushrooms, onions, and green peppers; one for plain cheese; and one for pepperoni. There were fifteen workers in each line. We used a measuring cup to measure out how much of each ingredient to put on a pizza so that we wouldn't run short at the end. It was tiring but rewarding work. We were standing in line for a five-hour shift. There were snacks like coffee, tea, and lemonade for anyone wanting to take a break. And afterward, supper was furnished for everyone. I don't think the supper was served until around 9 P.M. So it was a very long day.

First Frost: The End of the Garden

I go out and pick everything that is left in the garden if I am pretty certain there is going to be a frost. If I see that the temperatures are really dropping, I'll even pick my green tomatoes. If the fruit or vegetable is on the plant, the frost will make it soft and ruin it. It's interesting, because I've had tomatoes outside on the table and the frost didn't bother those, but it hurt the ones on the plants.

Usually, there is a frost here by the end of September, although some years it doesn't happen until well into October. In anticipation of the first frost, we clear the garden out and get it all tilled so that when spring comes Joe can just go out and retill it. Joe likes to haul manure out to the garden before he tills it. Dad always said you should have your garden plowed in the fall so that the fertilizer has all winter to work into the soil. For fertilizer I put everything in there, including piles of kitchen waste, and then Joe tills it under. It really helps the soil.

Once the pizzas were done, they were boxed up and carried up a ramp to a freezer truck where they sat overnight for delivery the next day. Teams of Amish delivery people rode in vans with non-Amish drivers to all the nearby church districts with the pizzas.

Whether it is a pizza drive or a submarine sandwich drive, the event is announced the week before in church and published in local Amish bulletins and publications. Everyone in the community will be expecting someone to drop by on the announced date with a pizza or sandwich in exchange for a donation. It's guesswork to figure out how many pizzas or sandwiches will be needed, since orders are not taken ahead of time!

There was a big sub drive in our community one year, and nothing had to be purchased; everything was donated by local businesses and church members. And because the sandwiches don't stay as fresh when they are frozen, they had to be assembled and delivered all in the same day.

The vegetables for the sandwiches were cut up the day before. Everyone began gathering at 2:30 A.M. to start assembling the sandwiches. I had just given birth to baby Kevin, so I couldn't go, but my sisters Verena, Susan, Emma, and Emma's husband, Jacob, went. They gathered in a church member's basement to put together the sandwiches. Everyone wore gloves to keep everything clean. There was shredded lettuce, green pepper slices, tomato slices, pickles, and meat and cheese. Everything was in little plastic sandwich bags and delivered—along with mayonnaise and mustard packets and the sub bread—as a "sandwich kit." As soon as the sandwich kits were done, drivers took off for the farthest away communities to begin deliveries. If vegetables were in short supply, women began peeling and slicing more and getting them ready to go. All the sandwiches were done and assembled around 8:30 or 9 A.M., and then everyone had breakfast. Food was brought in, but some were eating sub sandwiches for breakfast.

It is announced in church ahead of time when a "drive" will be held and a sheet of paper is passed around where volunteers sign up for whatever shift and job they'd like to have.

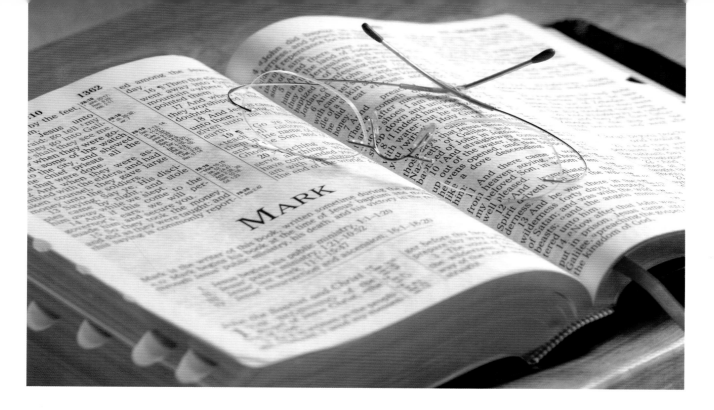

Weddings

In the Amish church, weddings seem to be held throughout the spring, summer, and fall. Fall seems to be an increasingly popular time to get married.

The new Amish settlement in Michigan that we live in does wedding meals differently in some ways than where we lived in Indiana. For one thing, all the children eat at the tables. Where we lived in Indiana, young children ate "help-yourself-style" at their own table. But here at our weddings in Michigan every child has his own place setting. Also, celery is used on the tables as decoration in Indiana, but that is not done around here.

The menu for our Indiana wedding meals almost always included "nothings," or "knee patches," which are sugar-sprinkled deep-fried circles of dough that are served stacked one on top of the another. But around here they have never heard of these desserts. Different communities do things in different ways.

Another thing they have a lot of around here that really helps with the big event are "wedding wagons." These are portable kitchens that can be hired to prepare all the wedding food. Several Amish own and rent out the kitchens as a part-time job.

The kitchens typically have five gas stoves in them, sinks, and cabinets along both sides of the wall. The cabinets contain all the dishes, stainless-steel kettles, and utensils needed to serve the hundreds of people that attend a typical wedding. The wagons are generator powered, with hot and cold running water, silverware, and over three hundred place settings, including coffee cups, glasses, and silverware. Most of them have a ramp for easy walking up and down. And a lot of times they have a cooler inside with shelves for the potato salads and things that need to be kept cool.

These wedding wagons are also used at funerals a lot. A large meal is usually served after someone's funeral (see page 140).

Our Wedding

I met Joe when was I was seventeen. He had a few sisters that moved into our church. Some of them married boys from our church. I met Joe through his sisters, and we just started dating. Our courtship lasted for five years.

I was nervous on our wedding morning. Even though it was July, it was such a cool morning and our wedding was set to be held in an outbuilding. Joe was in bad shape; he was so nervous.

It was a big wedding with close to seven hundred in attendance. The menu was fried chicken, mashed potatoes, gravy, noodles, and numerous side dishes and several varieties of pies: just a regular wedding menu.

When we came in to Mom and Dad's house after being married, the wedding cooks laid a broom flat on the floor in front of the door. They told me later that if I had stepped over it I was going to be a lazy housewife. If I picked it up, I wouldn't be lazy. Turns out I did pick it up, I didn't want anyone to trip over it.

When each of us children got married, Mom and Dad gave us a big hog and a young milking cow so we would have our meat and milk. They did this for all of their children after they married. They were very loving and generous in this way. All the boys, for instance, got a horse and buggy from Mom and Dad when they turned twenty-one. We girls got a cupboard, table, and chairs.

And when it was time to move into our first home, Mom thought of everything we could possibly need to give us a start: baking powder, baking soda, spices, meat she had canned herself, vegetables. It made it really nice to start off our married life together with all of these supplies.

HOMEMADE CHEESE SPREAD
Serves 110 to 130

This is a spread that is served at a lot of meals after church. It's good on a piece of bread or served as a sandwich.

6½ to 7 cups milk
2 (10-ounce) cans evaporated milk
1 pound butter, softened
8 pounds American cheese, cut into 1-inch cubes
1 (16-ounce) box Velveeta cheese, cut into 1-inch cubes

Preheat the oven to 250°F. Put all the ingredients in a roasting pan and bake, stirring every 15 minutes, until melted and smooth. Remove from the oven and serve as a sandwich spread. Cover and refrigerate any leftovers.

Kevin's note: Amish weddings, like most of their customs, vary from place to place in exact execution. But typically, the ceremony begins around 9 A.M. The service lasts 2½ to 3 hours, and is entirely spoken in Pennsylvania Dutch. The service is usually held at the homestead of the bride-to-be. Brides will often wear a royal blue dress with a white cape. Some Amish grooms wear neckties, the only day in their life that they'll adorn themselves with this apparel. The service ends around noon and is followed with a feast for all in attendance.

FUNERALS

Perhaps one of the most endearing and inspiring traits of the Amish is their steadfast faith. I've attended three or four Amish funerals in my lifetime, and each one is punctuated by an awe-inspiring stoicism and firm belief that the deceased has passed on to a better place.

At Elizabeth Coblentz's funeral, while I was besieged with a deep grief, I found myself being comforted by her children when it should have been the other way around. But their faith was so firm that Elizabeth had passed on to be with their father, Ben, that their grief was tempered by this knowledge.

Amish funerals are well-organized events that pay tribute to the deceased while celebrating the gift of life.

Even the most conservative Amish practice embalming. Once the body is returned from a local funeral home, a visitation is held at the home of the deceased. Sometimes the visitation will last up to forty-eight hours to allow faraway visitors to have time to come and pay their final respects. At least a few family members or relatives will stay with the body throughout the event. Many Europeans once practiced the ritual of a twenty-four-hour vigil, and this is a variation on that custom. The coffins are simple, usually locally constructed plywood boxes. The Amish prefer to die as they live, plainly, without frills or vanity. People walk by the open casket at the visitation to briefly pay their respects.

The day after the visitation, a funeral service is held. Like all Amish religious observances, this service is conducted in the home. Church benches are set up around the coffin, and a minister delivers a sermon. According to Amish custom, the service is in Pennsylvania

Dutch. The casket is sealed and loaded onto a cart to be pulled by a buggy. The procession slowly heads to a nearby Amish cemetery. There are no headstones or flowers at the cemetery, just wooden grave-markers etched with the initials of the deceased and the dates of their birth and death. A simple graveside ceremony takes place, and then everyone heads back for a large meal. Sadness is usually replaced by smiles and a general sense of acceptance that the person has passed to a better beyond.

FUNERAL PIE
Serves 8

This raisin pie is a funeral tradition in Pennsylvania Amish communities, where the thick pie is a comfort for the grieving family. In other Amish communities, like Lovina's, a raisin pie is served at more celebratory occasions, like weddings.

2 cups raisins

2 cups water

½ cup packed light brown sugar

½ cup granulated sugar

3 tablespoons cornstarch

1½ teaspoons ground cinnamon

¼ teaspoon ground allspice

Pinch of salt

1 tablespoon apple cider vinegar

3 tablespoons butter

2 disks My Homemade Pie Dough (page 125)

Preheat the oven to 400°F.

Put the raisins and ⅔ cup of the water in a medium saucepan and heat over medium heat for 5 minutes.

Combine the sugars, cornstarch, spices, and salt in a medium bowl and, stirring constantly, gradually add the remaining 1⅓ cups water. Add this mixture to the raisins. Cook and stir until the mixture starts to bubble. Add the vinegar and butter and heat until the butter is melted. Remove from the oven and let cool until just warm.

Roll out 1 disk of dough to a ⅛-inch thickness on a floured surface. Line a 9-inch pie pan with the dough. Trim to a ½-inch overhang. Pour the filling into the crust. Roll out the second disk of dough, place on top of the pie, and trim to a to a 1-inch overhang. Fold the dough under and crimp the edge. Cut decorative slash marks into the top crust. Bake until golden brown, about 15 minutes. Remove from the oven and let cool completely.

LATE AUTUMN

With the garden done for the year, our attention begins to turn to other activities: hunting, butchering our old broth chickens, making sure we have enough coal for the winter ahead, and helping the children with the increasing homework assignments from their school.

HALLOWEEN

Unlike most calendar occasions that have wide observational variations between Amish settlements, Halloween is almost universally ignored. Some teenagers may go out and commit trickery, like soaping down someone's windows or toilet-papering a yard. Going door to door and collecting candy is not a common practice among the Amish. Occasionally an Amish child who attends public school might participate by dressing in costume, but never in one that would depict violence or an antireligious theme.

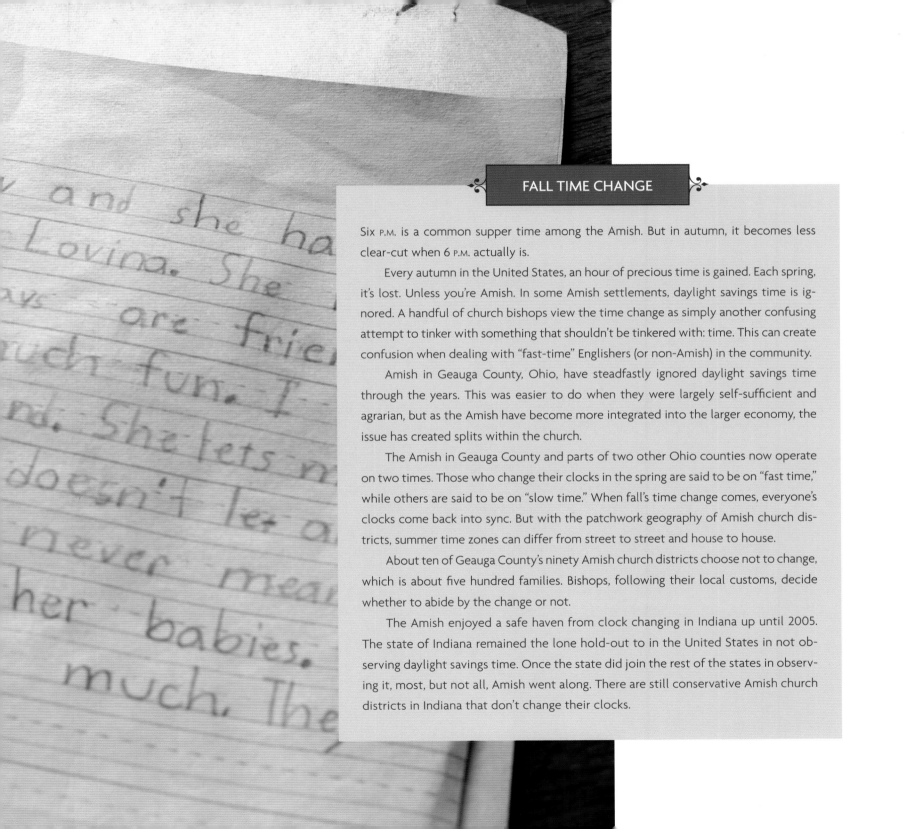

FALL TIME CHANGE

Six P.M. is a common supper time among the Amish. But in autumn, it becomes less clear-cut when 6 P.M. actually is.

Every autumn in the United States, an hour of precious time is gained. Each spring, it's lost. Unless you're Amish. In some Amish settlements, daylight savings time is ignored. A handful of church bishops view the time change as simply another confusing attempt to tinker with something that shouldn't be tinkered with: time. This can create confusion when dealing with "fast-time" Englishers (or non-Amish) in the community.

Amish in Geauga County, Ohio, have steadfastly ignored daylight savings time through the years. This was easier to do when they were largely self-sufficient and agrarian, but as the Amish have become more integrated into the larger economy, the issue has created splits within the church.

The Amish in Geauga County and parts of two other Ohio counties now operate on two times. Those who change their clocks in the spring are said to be on "fast time," while others are said to be on "slow time." When fall's time change comes, everyone's clocks come back into sync. But with the patchwork geography of Amish church districts, summer time zones can differ from street to street and house to house.

About ten of Geauga County's ninety Amish church districts choose not to change, which is about five hundred families. Bishops, following their local customs, decide whether to abide by the change or not.

The Amish enjoyed a safe haven from clock changing in Indiana up until 2005. The state of Indiana remained the lone hold-out to in the United States in not observing daylight savings time. Once the state did join the rest of the states in observing it, most, but not all, Amish went along. There are still conservative Amish church districts in Indiana that don't change their clocks.

HUNTING

Autumn is hunting season in many Amish communities. The harvesting is done for the year, and it's a good time to stock up on meat for the winter.

Joe started hunting with his father when he was thirteen or fourteen. He started with pheasants, but he could never hit them. He finally figured out that he was using the wrong eye to sight them. Once he got that problem corrected he could hit them! Joe still enjoys hunting, but he often doesn't get time to do it. He hunted more in Indiana when he could just walk into Mom and Dad's woods and go. Joe's favorite game to hunt for is deer, but he'll also hunt squirrels and rabbits on occasion.

One time, Joe went hunting and sat on the ground beside a tree. He got so tired that he fell asleep, and when he woke up there were deer tracks right in front of him.

Joe especially loves deer steak fried with eggs and potatoes. The only deer meat that I'll really eat is summer sausage. I guess I'm like my father. He was never really a big fan about anything wild. My dad said by the time you went through the trouble to get your hunting license, you might as well just buy the meat.

Someday, Joe will take Benjamin and Joseph hunting. But before he does he wants to take them to hunting classes. They really encourage that among the Amish around here. The classes seem like a really good thing unless you know a lot about guns and can teach them yourself. They had lessons around here this year, but Joe won't let them go until they are quite a bit older. The idea of hunting accidents really scares me, so I'll feel a bit better when the boys are older and have taken classes.

VENISON SAUSAGE
Serves 8

Deer meat is a highlight of the fall hunting season. The children get so excited to see their dad come out of the woods after a successful hunt. Deer meat, or venison, can be used in so many different ways: steaks, burgers, stews, soups, jerky, casseroles, and one of our favorites, sausage. This recipe is a big hit in our household.

¼ teaspoon garlic powder
1 tablespoon mustard seed
½ teaspoon liquid smoke
¼ onion salt
3 tablespoons salt
4 teaspoons black pepper
1 cup cold water
2 pounds venison, ground

In a large bowl, mix all the spices with the water and the liquid smoke. Then add the meat and mix well. Form into two loaves and wrap them in foil with the shiny side next to the meat. Place the loaves in the refrigerator for 48 hours. Remove from the refrigerator and, using a butter knife, make 5 small slashes in each loaf. Place the loaves in a large pot and cover with cold water. Bring to a boil. Decrease the heat and simmer uncovered for 1½ hours. Remove the loaves from the water and let cool. Rewrap in new foil and refrigerate for 12 hours, then cut and enjoy.

CHICKEN

We usually butcher chickens twice a year, in the spring and in the fall. The autumn butchering is for the older hens that give us that all-important chicken broth, which we use mainly for homemade chicken noodle soup and gravies.

This twice-yearly butchering of chickens has been a part of my life for as long as I can remember, and now the tradition and chore is being passed down to my children. Our children help with the cleaning after the chickens are butchered. They will reach in with their hands pull the innards out.

We will butcher around thirty chickens a year. The older hens have supplied us with eggs for several years before we butcher them, so we usually have a good supply of fresh eggs here. The broiler hens are butchered when they are around four or five pounds. That is when the meat is most tender. With older hens, the meat isn't as good, but it has more fat, which makes excellent broth once you cook the meat off the bones.

For the broiler chickens, we do not skin them; we want to keep the skin on. A broiler takes a lot longer to butcher because we have to pluck the feathers. We eat the skin of these chickens, so we want every feather off. We used to always pluck the chickens by hand, but have in recent years switched to a gasoline-powered motorized "plucker" with rubber arms that spin around and take most of the feathers off, though it is still a lot of work. The older chickens are just used to make broth, so they don't require as much work and care in cutting. We don't need the skin kept on these, so we just hang the chicken on a nail, cut the skin in half, and pull it off.

It is a bit of science education for our children to see the insides of an animal. For instance, one of the things you see when gutting a chicken is an egg sack that can sometimes contain yolks without a shell. Some in the older generations still salvage those and boil and fry them, but I usually don't. Other people keep the chicken feet and clean and fry those, but I throw them away. I just don't care for that part. We do keep the gizzard and the heart. We like fried gizzards. Joe will keep the liver to use for bait if he is going fishing.

I can the chicken broth for later use. I make homemade chicken noodle soup a lot. I don't follow a recipe, I just sort of make it by feel, putting in a little bit of this and that. I open a quart of homemade broth, put it in a pan, and add some water. Then I bring it to a boil. After it is boiling, I will add my noodles. Sometimes I dice a few carrots in. I have put potatoes in before, but most of the time it is just noodles.

Chicken noodle soup is almost always served at lunch break during Communion services. Communion church is held twice a year and lasts much longer than our regular 2½-hour service. In addition, chicken noodle soup is typically served at every church service meal for the little ones who aren't old enough to eat sandwiches. Usually there is a big pot of chicken noodle soup for the little ones at the service.

Chicken-butchering time gives our family good working time together and provides us with many meals in the months ahead. I'll share some of our favorite chicken recipes!

CHICKEN GRAVY

Makes 6 cups

This is our favorite homemade gravy to use on mashed potatoes and baked chicken. I use the broth from our chickens to make the gravy. I don't always fix it this way; many times I don't put in the egg. But at weddings around here they use eggs because adding them helps thicken the gravy, which people seem to like. My job at one wedding was, along with another lady, to make all the gravy. I think we made two 3-gallon pots of gravy that day.

4½ cups chicken broth

1½ tablespoons chicken soup base

Small pinch of garlic salt

5 tablespoons instant Clear Gel

2 tablespoons all-purpose flour

½ cup milk

1 large egg, slightly beaten

Combine the broth, soup base, and garlic salt in a medium saucepan. Bring to a boil. Mix the Clear Jel, flour, and ¼ cup of the milk together in a small bowl and stir into the broth mixture. Add the egg and the remaining ¼ cup milk. Gradually whisk into the hot broth and whisk until thickened.

CHEESY CHICKEN CHOWDER
Serves 4 to 6

This is a delicious, hearty meal for those first cold autumn days. Sometimes I will use 3 tablespoons of cornstarch instead of flour as a thickener for this because it takes less and makes the soup smoother than the flour does. This is a very thick soup. Sometimes as a variation I will stick it in the oven instead and bake it just like a casserole. It is even thicker when prepared that way. This is something everyone in our family really enjoys.

1 onion, chopped

1 cup chopped carrots

1 cup diced potatoes

1 cup diced celery

4 cups water

5 cups diced cooked chicken

4 tablespoons butter

6 tablespoons all-purpose flour

2 cups milk

1 cup shredded Cheddar or mozzarella cheese

1 teaspoon salt

Combine the vegetables and water in a soup pot and bring to a boil; reduce the heat to medium and cook until soft, about 20 minutes. Add the chicken and butter. Stir in the flour, then gradually stir in the milk. Add the cheese and salt and stir until the cheese is melted. Spoon into bowls and serve.

CHICKEN POTPIE

Serves 4 to 6

Some Amish recipes for potpie resemble a soup with bits of dough in it. This recipe, though, is more like a homemade version of the potpies found frozen in the supermarkets.

2 cups diced peeled potatoes

1¾ cups sliced carrots

1 cup (2 sticks) butter

⅔ cup chopped onion

1 cup all-purpose flour

1¾ teaspoons salt

¾ teaspoon ground pepper

2 tablespoons chicken soup base

3 cups chicken broth

1½ cups milk

4 cups cubed cooked chicken

1 cup frozen or fresh green peas

4 disks My Homemade Pie Dough
(page 125)

Combine the potatoes and carrots in a large saucepan. Cover with water and boil until almost tender, 12 to 15 minutes. Drain and set aside.

Melt the butter in a large saucepan over medium heat and sauté the onion until tender, about 5 minutes. Stir in the flour, salt, pepper, and chicken soup base until blended. Gradually whisk in the broth and milk. Bring to a boil and cook, whisking constantly, until thick, about 2 minutes. Stir in the chicken, peas, potatoes, and carrots. Remove from the heat.

Roll out 2 disks of pastry to a ⅛-inch thickness. Line two 9-inch pie pans with the pastry and trim to a ½-inch overhang. Spoon the chicken mixture into the pastry shells. Roll out 2 more pastry disks to a ⅛-inch thickness. Cover the pie pans with the pastry and trim to a 1-inch overhang. Fold the dough under and crimp the edges. Cut decorative slashes in the tops of the pies. Bake until golden brown, about 30 minutes.

Note: The My Homemade Pie Dough makes 6 disks of dough, which is two more than you need here. The two leftover disks can be refrigerated for a few days or frozen for several months and used in another recipe.

EASY CHICKEN CASSEROLE

Serves 6

The children and Joe really go for this. If I go too long without fixing this, Joe will start asking me when I'm going to fix it again. I like to fix a whole cake pan full of this. I kind of go by feel; I add a little more of this and that to make a meal for us. As a variation, if I don't have cream of chicken soup on hand, I'll use cream of mushroom. It still tastes great!

½ cup (1 stick) margarine or butter

⅓ cup all-purpose flour

1 cup milk

2 cups chicken broth

1½ teaspoons salt

½ teaspoon pepper

1 (3-ounce) can mushrooms, or 3 ounces fresh mushrooms

2 cups cubed cooked chicken

8 ounces noodles, cooked and drained

⅓ cup grated Parmesan cheese

Preheat the oven to 350°F. Grease an 8-cup casserole.

Melt the margarine in a medium saucepan over low heat, then whisk in the flour until smooth. Gradually whisk the milk, then the broth, and cook until thickened. Stir in the salt, pepper, and mushrooms. Add the chicken, cooked noodles, and cheese.

Spoon the mixture into the prepared dish. Bake until bubbly and golden, about 45 minutes.

CHICKEN AND DUMPLINGS

Serves 4 to 6

Chicken and homemade dumplings is one of my favorites. The children like to drop the dumplings into the broth, so it is a good family meal to fix together.

DUMPLINGS

2 cups all-purpose flour

1 teaspoon salt

½ teaspoon baking powder

6 tablespoons margarine or butter, melted

1 large egg, beaten

½ cup milk

2 boneless, skinless chicken breast halves

2 (10¾-ounce) cans cream of chicken soup

To make the dumplings: Combine the flour, salt, and baking powder in a large bowl. Stir with a whisk to blend. Stir in the melted margarine, egg, and milk until a smooth, soft dough forms. Roll out to a ½- to ¾-inch thickness on a floured surface and cut into 1-inch squares.

Place the chicken in a medium saucepan, add enough water to cover the chicken, and simmer over medium-high heat until the chicken is cooked through. Cool, drain the water, and cut up the chicken into bite-sized pieces. Combine the chicken pieces and soup in a large pot and simmer until tender, about 30 minutes. Add the dumplings one at a time. Simmer for 5 more minutes and then serve.

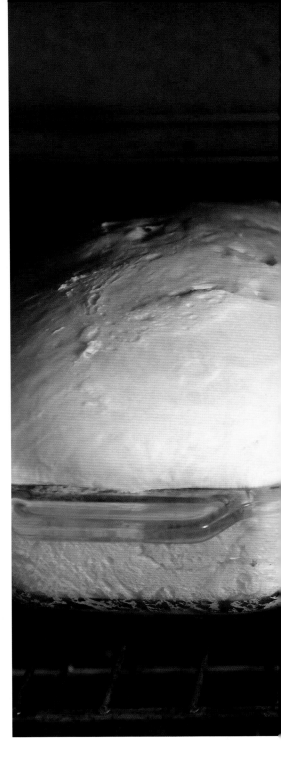

SOURDOUGH BREAD

It just seems we don't eat heavy home-baked breads during the summer months so much. So when the weather begins to cool, we really enjoy homemade sourdough treats like cinnamon rolls and breads. I never made sourdough bread until years after Joe and I were married. Then someone from church gave me a "starter" recipe, and now I make sourdough bread, cinnamon rolls, and other treats with it. There are many different variations of starters that exist. The one I use is more of a liquid. So if your starter looks "liquidy," then you are on the right track.

153

SOURDOUGH STARTER

You can either get a cup of starter from someone who has some and just skip to the "starter feed" section of the instructions, or you can begin from scratch. Either way, this takes some time and trial and error to get it right, but once you do it it is definitely worthwhile!

3 packages active dry yeast
1 cup warm water (105° to 115°F)

STARTER FEED
¾ cup sugar
3 tablespoons instant potatoes
1 cup warm water (105° to 115°F)

To make the starter: Mix the yeast and warm water in a small bowl. Put into a plastic container, seal, and refrigerate for 3 to 5 days.

To make the starter feed: Combine the sugar, potatoes, and water in a small bowl and stir into the starter. Cover loosely (to allow some of the pressure to escape as the gases build) and let stand at room temperature for 5 to 12 hours. The mixture will be bubbly.

Take out 1 cup to make bread and loosely cover the starter and return it to the refrigerator. Feed again after 3 to 5 days. If not making bread after feeding the starter, throw away 1 cup to avoid depleting the starter. **Note:** Do not put the lid on tight.

SOURDOUGH BREAD

Makes 3 loaves

Sourdough bread is something new for us. We didn't eat it growing up, but after we moved to Michigan I discovered that a lot of the Amish women in this area make sourdough breads, so it was fun to learn a new type of baking.

2 tablespoons sugar

½ cup olive oil

1 teaspoon salt

1½ cups warm water (105° to 115°F)

6 cups bread flour

1 cup Sourdough Starter (page 154)

3 teaspoons butter, melted

Combine the sugar, oil, salt, water, flour, and starter in a large bowl. Stir to make a dough. Form the dough into a ball. Grease another large bowl. Put the dough in and turn to coat. Cover with waxed paper and let stand overnight. (Do not refrigerate.)

The next morning, punch the dough down and divide it into thirds. (If you are making Sourdough Cinnamon Rolls, page 157, punch the dough down and divide it in half.) Knead each part on a floured surface 8 to 10 times. Grease three 8½ by 4½-inch loaf pans and turn each loaf over in the pan to coat. Cover with waxed paper and let rise in the pans until it is just above the rims of the pans, 4 or 5 hours. Preheat the oven to 350°F. Bake the bread until the crust is nice and golden brown, 30 to 35 minutes. Remove from the oven and brush each loaf with 1 teaspoon of the butter. Unmold and let cool on wire racks.

SOURDOUGH CINNAMON ROLLS

Makes 24 large rolls

I didn't realize that you could make cinnamon rolls with sourdough. The sourdough cinnamon rolls are a lot easier than when you mix up a batch from scratch, because I've already got the dough on hand. My family all loves cinnamon rolls and they can hardly wait to eat them. I ice them with my homemade icing. I don't like store-bought icing on mine; I like to make my own. Sometimes I put a limit on how many cinnamon rolls the family can eat, or they'll just keep eating them.

Sourdough Bread dough, prepared through first rise (page 155)
6 tablespoons margarine or butter, softened
1 cup packed brown sugar
3 teaspoons ground cinnamon

ICING
⅓ cup margarine or butter, softened
1 teaspoon vanilla extract
4 cups sifted powdered sugar
½ cup milk

After the dough has risen overnight, punch it down, divide it in half, and form two balls of dough. Take a ball of dough and roll it out as thin as possible on a floured surface. Brush the dough with half of the melted margarine. Sprinkle half of the brown sugar evenly over the dough, then sprinkle with half of the cinnamon.

Roll up the dough like a jelly roll. Cut each roll into slices ½ to ¾ inch thick. Place the slices ½ inch apart in a buttered jelly roll pan, cover with waxed paper. Repeat with the remaining ball of dough and remaining margarine, brown sugar, and cinnamon. Let rise for 4 hours.

Preheat the oven to 350°F. Bake the rolls until golden brown, about 20 minutes. Remove from the oven and let cool slightly while making the icing: Cream the margarine with the vanilla and 1 cup of the powdered sugar in a medium bowl. Gradually add the milk and the remaining powdered sugar and stir until smooth. Drizzle over the warm cinnamon rolls and serve immediately.

Thanksgiving

Out in Indiana, we would sometimes use the day to get the garden plowed before winter. Here in Michigan, we spend Thanksgiving morning fasting and in prayer, sort of like Good Friday.

We always had turkey and pumpkin pie on the menu on this day when I was growing up. I always do the same for my family. Sometimes I use an oven bag for the turkey; I think it tastes better and keeps the turkey juicier. Turkey once or twice a year is enough for me; it is not something we eat very often.

HOMEMADE DRESSING
Serves 6

We call this dish dressing when it is served in a serving dish, but we call it stuffing when it is stuffed into a turkey. I just bake my dressing, but Mom would always fry it in a pan. I like mine better baked, because it's not as greasy.

2 tablespoons chicken soup base

2 cups hot water

4 large eggs, beaten

¼ cup diced carrot

¼ cup diced celery

¼ cup chopped yellow onion

2 cups hot water (or use potato water for better flavor)

10 slices bread, crumbled

1 teaspoon seasoning salt

Preheat the oven to 350°F. Grease an 8-cup casserole dish or cake pan.

Dissolve the soup base in the water. Add all the remaining ingredients and mix well. Pour into the prepared dish and bake for 40 to 45 minutes.

We are always a little sad to see autumn come to an end.
We savor those last warm days of being barefoot
with the sun's rays on our backs, and look toward the
winter with a bit of dread. Will it be long, cold, and snowy?
Only our Creator knows for certain.

winter

For the New Year give me what is Thine, namely Thy great, new heavenly comfort, forgiveness of all my sins which I have committed this past year and from my youth, and Thy Holy Spirit and eternal life.

—Excerpt from Amish New Year's prayer

From our house I have a great view in all four directions.

On wintry days, I can really see the blowing snow whipped up by the winds. When Joe and the children are home from work and school because of the drifted-over roads it makes me feel good that everyone is safe and warm at home. Sometimes, the snow swirls so fast it is hard to see anything. But our toasty gaslights inside throw off a lot of heat and brightness. It always seems cozy in here, even during the worst winter weather. Winter evenings are spent inside reading, playing games, working puzzles, and sipping hot cocoa, which makes the snowstorms outside almost enjoyable. In addition to hot cocoa, we enjoy hearty meat dishes, delicious once-a-year holiday food treats, and the winter treat of home-made ice cream!

Along with the snows of winter come the holidays, and with them many family gatherings. Even though the gatherings are enjoyable to attend, I am always relieved once they are over because it is nice when everything slows down a little.

I am always filled with a little dread when winter begins approaching us. Months of work—harvesting, canning, stocking up on firewood and other fuel—goes into preparing for winter. The outdoor chores have to be wrapped up, like getting the gardens cleared and tilled and the leaves raked before that first snowfall. On the good side, it does seem like I have a little more time to catch up on mending and sewing during the winter months.

While the garden is taking its winter slumber, there are plenty of other chores to do during the cold months. For instance, we do our once-a-year butchering of beef and pork during the winter, usually during February. The work can be hot and messy, not a chore you'd want to tackle during the summer months. The beef needs to be chilled before it's cut, and this is much easier to do on cold winter days.

WHY I LIKE WINTER
by Susan, age eleven

Winter is my favorite season of the year. I enjoy the snow and I like playing in it. My brothers and sisters and I like to make snowmen, snow angels, and igloos. We like pulling each other on the sleds over the snow. Most of all I like when Dad puts our pony, Stormy, to the sled and pulls us around. I like taking sled rides down the hill. Another thing I like: There are hardly ever thunderstorms and tornadoes in the winter. I hate those storms and they always scare me.

I like winter because we can make ice cream, and I also like having Christmas and my birthday. I like not having to mow grass and weed the garden. That is why winter is my favorite season of the year!

HOLIDAYS
AND CELEBRATIONS

The holidays are a busy but joyful time for us. The house begins to fill with the scent of homemade fudge, peanut brittle, cookies, and other Christmas candy. The children begin to get excited at the thought of receiving gifts. But we always remind the children of the reason for the season: to celebrate the birth of Christ. We don't like for that to get lost in all the activity. We also miss our dearly departed loved ones around the holidays but take comfort in knowing that they are in a better place.

Christmas with the Eichers: Gifts and Gatherings

We try to make Christmas morning exciting for the children while still honoring Christ's birth.

A lot of the Amish don't recognize Santa. Our kids know there isn't one; we always tell them he isn't real, but we still have fun teasing about Santa Claus coming. Some Amish want to teach their kids about Santa, others don't. Sometimes the children will write letters to Santa in school, but they know he is just a fun make-believe character of the season. I know I was heartbroken when I found out there wasn't a Santa, so I don't teach my children that he is real.

Gifts

There are many special memories through the years of treasured gifts given and received.

On Christmas morning, I have all the children's gifts wrapped. We then pass them out to each one. Sometimes, we take our time and everyone unwraps one at a time and we'll help them if it is a toy that needs to be put together. I'll start breakfast and we'll enjoy more of a brunch. The children are usually so excited that they can hardly eat until later anyway.

Mom and Dad never wrapped the gifts. They hid them until Christmas morning. We children would come downstairs to the breakfast table. Mom would put our plates on the table filled with candy and maybe an orange. And our gifts would be out so when we woke up we would find them.

We try to give our children special Christmas gifts that they'll remember for years. For instance, we give gifts of books and maybe a Bible to each child.

For our younger children, we might buy them some games. Sometimes we also give the youngest children an Amish-dressed doll or the boys toys of farm animals and a farm set. As the children get older, we try to get them more practical gifts or ones that they'll use for years. For instance, one year when Susan was eleven we gave her some bookends to begin her book collection. Another year, when our daughter Elizabeth was twelve, Joe and I gave her a shelf to hang on the wall in her room. We try to give each of the girls a small hope chest when they get into their early teens so they can begin to keep special items. Around age fifteen or sixteen we try to get the girls a dinnerware set. And when they get older a small piece of furniture, perhaps a recliner or rocker, to put into their bedrooms.

Joe surprised me one year with a nice big stainless-steel skillet for Christmas. It was something I could really use. One year, I got Joe a saw. I had my brother-in-law Jacob get it for me and Joe was really surprised. When I was seventeen, Mom and Dad gave me a cedar chest, and for my sixteenth birthday I got a dinnerware set.

A NONCOMMERCIAL CHRISTMAS

A visit to an Amish home around the holidays is notable because of what one *doesn't* see.

There is no Christmas tree festooned with bright lights and gaudy ornaments. There are no yards glittering with lights, stockings hanging from the mantel, or candles in the windows. You won't find a plate of homemade chocolate cookies for Kris Kringle waiting by the fireplace on Christmas Eve. There are no harried trips to the shopping mall or sifting through a mound of mail-order catalogs. Unless the holiday falls on a Sunday, there are no special Christmas church services.

The absence of all these typical holiday signs doesn't mean that the Amish aren't observing the occasion. Christ's birthday is, along with Easter, the most sacred occasion on the Amish religious calendar. The Amish are busy with the holidays just like everyone else; they're just observing them in their own quiet, subdued way.

One of the few outward ways that the Amish do celebrate the season is with food. A whole host of special goodies makes its way onto menus only at this time of year. Rich and mulitflavored fudges, homemade peanut brittle, handmade chocolate candies, and brightly iced Christmas cookies in the secular shapes of bells, reindeer, and sleighs make the kitchen a more festive place. Often, these candies and baked goods are given to family and friends as Christmas presents. The exchanging of other gifts varies greatly depending on the local church rules. Many Amish do exchange presents for Christmas, but they are often handmade and homemade gifts. A husband might make a special kitchen shelf for his wife, while a wife might make a fine Sunday shirt for her husband. But there are also Amish who will venture into discount department stores to buy more mainstream gifts for their loved ones. This is especially true when it comes to purchasing toys as gifts for youngsters. Children are children no matter what culture or creed, and toys are always treasured.

As a general rule, Amish children are less materialistic than those of other Western cultures. An illustration of this occurred when Lovina and her family were preparing to move into their newly constructed home in Michigan shortly after Christmas in 2006. The Eicher children all happily agreed to put off receiving Christmas gifts so that everyone could focus on moving into the new home, which was present enough for all.

Some Amish parents do include secular figures like Santa Claus in Christmas celebrations, while others do not. This again varies greatly depending on local custom and parental preference.

Sending Christmas cards is another activity that some Amish homemakers jump into with great zest. Sometimes the cards will be homemade, sometimes store-bought. With huge families and lots of news to share, the number of cards sent out can go into the triple digits.

GATHERINGS

Our church has an annual Christmas potluck supper after the Sunday services that fall before the holiday, which is one way the congregation marks the occasion. Early in December at church we will pass a paper around and everyone puts down what they are going to bring so we don't end up with all casseroles, desserts, or salads. There is a section of the paper reserved for each type of food. We usually end up with a big table full of food. And there are two lines, one for the men and one for the women. Young children will go through the line with either parent.

In our family, we have traditionally gathered together for the holidays, all my brothers and sisters and parents (when they were still with us) in one place. Usually, the gathering would be held on New Year's Day, because trying to get everyone together on Christmas as families grew and got older was more difficult. Sometimes now we even hold the "Christmas gathering" in mid-January.

We have many recipes that are favorites around the holidays. Fudge is one that really goes over well around here!

SOUR CREAM CUT-OUT COOKIES

Makes about 18 cookies, depending on shapes

This is an easy Christmas cookie that the kids like to cut out and decorate. It takes a lot longer when they help, but they enjoy it. Some of the shapes we cut them into include a Christmas tree and a bell. Sometimes I have to watch the younger children, as they like to eat the dough. But with the raw eggs in there I don't like them to.

1 cup (2 sticks) butter, softened

1½ cups sugar

3 large eggs, beaten

1 cup sour cream

2 tablespoons vanilla extract

3½ to 4 cups all-purpose flour

2 teaspoons baking powder

1 teaspoon baking soda

FROSTING

⅓ cup shortening

1 teaspoon vanilla

4 cups powdered sugar

½ cup milk

Food coloring (optional)

Colored sprinkles, for decorating (optional)

Chocolate chips, for decorating (optional)

Preheat the oven to 350°F. Lightly grease a baking sheet.

Cream the butter and sugar together in a large bowl. Stir in the eggs, sour cream, and vanilla. Combine the flour, baking powder, and baking soda in a medium bowl and stir with a whisk to blend. Add the dry ingredients to the wet ingredients and stir until a soft, firm dough is formed. Roll the dough out to a ½-inch thickness on a floured surface. Use your favorite shaped cookie cutters to cut out the dough. Place the shapes on the prepared pan.

Bake until golden brown around the edges, about 10 minutes. Remove from the oven and let cool on the pan for 5 minutes, then transfer to wire racks to cool completely.

To make the frosting: Cream the shortening with the vanilla and 1 cup of the powdered sugar. Gradually add the milk and the rest of the powdered sugar, beating constantly. More powdered sugar can be added to give you your desired thickness. Food coloring can also be added if you like. Spread the frosting on the cookies and decorate with colored sprinkles or chocolate chips. Let the frosting set before storing.

HOLIDAY FUDGE

Makes 64 pieces

When I was growing up, I always knew when the holidays were getting close because that is when fudge started appearing in the kitchen. Mom always made fudge for the holidays. I think my favorite kind is chocolate fudge. I find that a tin full of homemade fudge is a great gift to give for Christmas. I don't fix it too much just to have around the house because I think it is too rich for the children. They like it, but it is just too sweet.

1 cup granulated sugar

1 cup packed brown sugar

2 tablespoons cornstarch

2 ounces semisweet chocolate, chopped,
   or 6 tablespoons unsweetened cocoa powder

½ cup heavy cream

3 tablespoons butter

1 teaspoon vanilla extract

1 cup walnut pieces (optional)

Combine the sugars, cornstarch, chocolate, and cream in a heavy, medium saucepan. Bring to a boil over medium heat and cook for 2½ minutes. Stir in the butter and vanilla. Remove from heat. Let cool to lukewarm and then beat with spoon until the mixture holds its shape. Stir in the nuts. Pour into a buttered 8-inch square pan and let cool. Refrigerate until set. Cut the fudge into 1-inch squares.

NOËL COOKIES

Makes 1 giant cookie or several smaller ones

One of our favorite parts of the holiday season is all the delicious baked goods that we enjoy only at this time of year. This is a colorful cookie that you can decorate to look bright and inviting. The batter is baked as one large cookie and can later be cut into pieces.

1 cup (2 sticks) butter, softened
1 cup sugar
2 large eggs
1 teaspoon vanilla extract
2 cups all-purpose flour, plus more for dusting

ICING
1 cup sifted powdered sugar
2 tablespoons milk

Colored sugar for decorating (optional)

Preheat the oven to 325°F. Grease and lightly flour a baking sheet.

Combine the butter, sugar, eggs, vanilla, and the 2 cups flour. Beat vigorously with a wooden spoon until smooth. Spread the dough to the edges of the prepared pan. Lightly dust with flour. Bake until the center is set and the edges begin to turn golden brown, 25 to 30 minutes. Remove from the oven and let cool completely.

To make the icing: Stir the powdered sugar and milk together until smooth.

Spread the icing on the cookie and sprinkle with colored sugar. Cut into squares or leave as one giant cookie.

POPCORN BALLS

Makes 12 to 18 popcorn balls

Popcorn balls are something we enjoy every Christmas season. Mom always put in red food coloring to make them pink in color. Just a more festive, holiday-type touch. Most of the time we ate them so fast that there weren't any leftovers to store. But if you have leftovers, you can do what Mom did and just put them in a plastic container.

1 cup sugar

¾ cup water

¼ teaspoon salt

¼ cup light corn syrup

½ teaspoon vanilla extract

½ teaspoon distilled white vinegar

10 cups popped corn (about ½ cup popcorn kernels)

Combine the sugar, water, salt, and syrup in a small saucepan. Bring to a boil over high heat and cook, stirring constantly, to the hard-ball stage, when the mixture forms a firm ball, at around 255°F on a candy thermometer. Add the vanilla and vinegar and continue cooking to the soft-crack stage, when the mixture begins to separate into firm but still flexible strings, at about 270°F on a candy thermometer.

Put the popcorn in a large bowl and pour the sugar mixture slowly over the popcorn. Stir well to coat every kernel. When the mixture has cooled enough to handle, press it into baseball-sized balls with your buttered hands.

CARAMEL CORN

Makes about 2 gallons

While we enjoyed the sweetened popcorn balls growing up, I think my children favor this cara-mel corn. I don't like them to eat it as much because the caramel gets stuck on and between their teeth. But most of the Amish around here really seem to enjoy making this recipe around the holidays.

1 cup (2 sticks) margarine or butter

2 cups packed brown sugar

½ cup light corn syrup

½ teaspoon salt

1 tablespoon baking soda

2 gallons popped corn (about 2 cups popcorn kernels)

Preheat the oven to 250°F.

Combine the margarine, brown sugar, corn syrup, and salt in a small saucepan. Bring to a boil over high heat and cook for 5 minutes. Add the baking soda and stir hard. Put the popcorn in a roasting pan. Pour the hot sugar mixture over the popcorn and stir well. Bake, stirring every 10 minutes, until corn is completely coated and turns golden brown, 30 to 40 minutes.

CINNAMON PUDDING

Serves 6

I remember when I was a little girl my older sister, Leah, would make cinnamon pudding. This is a good recipe to fix around the holidays when company comes. The pudding looks like little pieces of cake, and it sort of has the taste of a cake and pudding together. We always serve it in a nice glass bowl.

SUGAR SYRUP

2 cups packed brown sugar

1½ cups water

2 tablespoons margarine or butter

About 3 cups all-purpose flour

1 cup granulated sugar

2 teaspoons baking powder

2 teaspoons ground cinnamon

1 cup milk

2 tablespoons margarine or butter

½ cup walnuts, chopped (optional)

2 cups sweetened whipped cream

Preheat the oven to 350°F. Grease a 9 by 13-inch pan.

To make the sugar syrup: Combine the brown sugar, water, and margarine in a small saucepan. Bring to a boil over medium heat, then remove from the heat. Set aside.

Combine the flour, granulated sugar, baking powder, and cinnamon in a large bowl. Stir with a whisk to blend. Stir in the milk and margarine to make a smooth batter. Spoon into the prepared pan and smooth the top. Pour the sugar syrup over the top and sprinkle evenly with the nuts.

Bake until the center is firm when you shake the pan a little, about 45 minutes. Cut into 1-inch squares and top each with a dollop of whipped cream.

PEANUT BRITTLE

Makes about 15 to 20 pieces

This is another recipe that we prepare only around the holidays. Mom would fix peanut brittle every Christmas that I can remember. My dad really liked homemade peanut brittle. And this is one of their holiday recipes. I fixed this recipe the first Christmas Joe and I were married.

2 cups sugar

1 cup light corn syrup

½ cup water

2 cups unsalted raw peanuts

2½ teaspoons baking soda

1 teaspoon butter

1 teaspoon vanilla extract

Combine the sugar, corn syrup, and water in a heavy, medium saucepan. Cook over medium heat, stirring constantly, until the sugar dissolves. Cook to the soft-ball stage, 235°F. Stir in the peanuts. Cook, stirring constantly, for 7 or 8 minutes to the hard-crack stage, 300°F.

Remove from the heat and stir in the baking soda, butter, and vanilla. Stir well and pour into a shallow, greased 9 by 13-inch baking dish. Let cool completely, then break into pieces about the size of a playing card.

Celebrating the New Year

We always celebrate the arrival of a new year in some way. On New Year's Eve, we usually have my sister Emma, her husband, Jacob, and their family come over, along with our sisters Susan and Verena. They might come in the afternoon for an early supper, maybe around 4 P.M. A typical New Year's Eve supper might consist of a pot roast, scalloped potatoes, baked beans, tossed salad, homemade sourdough bread, cheese, potato salad, and desserts. One year we barbecued chicken out on the grill because it was so nice outside, quite unusual for December 31!

Later on, we play games and eat snacks. Then we do the dishes, but we'll make it fun for the children. For instance, one year our children set the timer for fifteen minutes to see if we could get all the dishes done. Then it is time to play some board games to pass the evening. We usually step outside a few minutes before midnight. We'll all be waiting outside in the moonlight for the thrill of the new year's arrival. It never seems like it is very long before we can hear fireworks in the nearby town.

One year, the little boys had all gone to bed and were all still sleeping when midnight came. We probably should have awakened them, but getting all those children

back to bed is difficult. Still, hours later, we regretted not waking them up, because at 5:30 A.M., the boys were up, shouting "Happy New Year!" and playing hide and seek. I think they were upset that we didn't wake them, and maybe we should have.

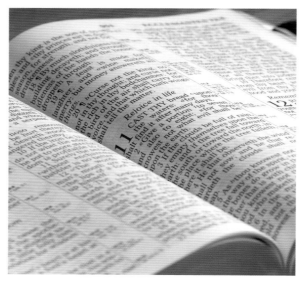

As we enter any new year, my mind is filled with thoughts of what lies ahead. On New Year's Day, it just seems a good time for a brand-new start, to try to have a better year than the one before. A new year is like turning a page.

We really don't make resolutions or goals, but like many Amish we have our traditions. For instance, picking a psalm is one of my favorite family traditions. For as long

as I can remember, on New Year's Day we get out the Bible and, with our eyes closed, each person points to a psalm. We've done that every year. Sometimes, we pick the psalms on Christmas Day in preparation for the new year. For example, one year I got a psalm telling me to be myself. It had forty-eight verses, which is a long psalm, which is taken to mean it may seem "like a long year." That same year, my daughter Elizabeth had fourteen verses in hers, so her year would seem to "go fast." One year, my husband, Joe, got a long psalm and he said that his year sure seemed long. Growing up, Mom would keep track of what psalm each child picked. So I've kept every psalm from when I was a baby. We tried to let baby Kevin pick a psalm this year, but he couldn't get the hang of it yet. Maybe next year.

New Year's Past

When I was a girl, my grandparents on my mother's side lived close, so we would always go visit them on New Year's Day. In fact, the entire extended family would gather there, which, counting all my Mom's siblings and their children, was quite a crowd. We would all assemble at Mom and Dad's house first and then go together—a huge group of us—over to my grandparents'.

They didn't live far away, so we could easily walk the stone and gravel road through the fields to get there. When we arrived, we would stand outside their door and sing "The New Year's Song." About halfway through, they'd open the door and let us all in. Then Grandma and Grandpa would sit in their rocking chairs to greet us all. We'd form a line with the younger ones first, and gradually each person would pass by them, give them a kiss on the cheek, and wish them a "Happy New Year!" After we had dinner, they'd stand by the end of the table with big cardboard boxes filled with little sacks of candy for all the children, plus a little dish. Mom would mark the year we were given the dish and save them all for us children, so I have a dish from every single year. They'd give all the eighty-one grandchildren the same thing, and then they would get their children some gifts also.

Food is an important part of celebrating New Year's Day, but there is not one single special dish. We eat all sorts of different things on New Year's Day. For instance, the only time Mom and Dad ever bought oranges and grapefruits or peanuts in shells would be for Christmas and New Year's Day; these were considered treats. We'd stand by the coal bucket and shell our peanuts, and the shells would burn in the fire.

THE NEW YEAR'S SONG

Musical instruments are not a part of Amish historical tradition. It's thought that instruments are frivolous, and that the way to connect with the Creator is through the simple beauty of the human voice. Some Amish men play harmonica, but that is the extent of instrumentals in their music.

Church services are punctuated by several songs sung out of a book known as the *Ausbund*. The *Ausbund*, with origins in the 1500s, is the oldest continually used hymnal in any Protestant faith.

While Christmas carols are not part of the Amish historical tradition, some secular songs like "Jingle Bells" may be sung by children. One holiday song that has deep roots within the Swiss Amish–Mennonite community that Lovina was born into, is a song known as "Neujahrslied." This is translated as "The New Year's Song," and is sung to welcome the arrival of a new calendar year. The song has its origins hundreds of years ago in Europe and is still sung today in Swiss Amish and Mennonite settlements in the United States. There are no Amish left in Europe; the last person of the Amish faith died in Alsace, France, in 1939.

"The New Year's Song" is sung in its original Swiss-German dialect, but its English translation is as follows:

'Tis time now to welcome the happy new year,
God grant you to live and enjoy the new year.
Good fortune and blessings to dwell in your home,
God grant you such blessings in this year in your home.
In heaven before the great heavenly throne,
God grant thee reward in that heavenly home.
In closing this year we repeat this one wish,
God grant you on high once that heavenly bliss.

NEWER NEW YEAR'S

It seems some of the older family traditions are fading away, but we are trying to replace them with new ones here in Michigan.

I remember one New Year's not long ago that was pretty typical of how we spend the holiday. We greeted the new year with a breakfast of burritos (page 9) In addition to that, we had chocolate milk, orange juice, grapefruit juice, coffee, tea, homemade sourdough bread, and lots of desserts.

After breakfast, we spent the rainy morning playing board games. The adults played the board game Aggravation, which is a favorite. Jacob and Emma were on a team, Joe and I were on one, and Verena and Susan were on another. While we played this game, the children played Connect Four and Sorry! After a morning full of games, we ate a taco supper around 2 P.M. Everyone was so full from breakfast, we just decided tacos would be a good, lighter meal. In addition, Emma brought a big bowl full of homemade potato salad.

One year, Emma and Jacob started for home around 4 P.M., and as they did, we saw an amazing rainbow that filled the sky. We weren't expecting this on New Year's Day. It just seemed like a lucky sign. The skies cleared and it was like a whole new start, a great way to begin the New Year.

SAUERKRAUT SUPPER

Serves 4 to 6

Sauerkraut is something that we enjoy in December and January. The cabbage is usually ready to harvest in the fall, and after I make it into sauerkraut, I usually let it sit in sealed containers in my cellar for two months to get that perfect taste. So, around New Year's Day it is ready. This is a good recipe to bring in the new year!

5 to 6 cups sauerkraut

2 to 3 cups water

1 teaspoon onion powder

1 teaspoon garlic powder

1 teaspoon sugar

1 teaspoon salt

½ teaspoon ground pepper

1 (2- to 3-pound) boneless pork
   roast

DUMPLINGS

2 cups Bisquick

1 cup water

Preheat the oven to 250°F.

   Rinse the sauerkraut and put it in a roasting pan. Add the water, then stir in the spices, sugar, salt, and pepper. Set the roast on top. Bake for 4 hours, or until tender. Remove the roast, let it cool, then cut into bite-sized pieces.

To make the dumplings: Mix the Bisquick and water together in a medium bowl. Place the roasting pan with the sauerkraut on the stovetop and bring to a slow boil. Drop the dumpling batter in spoonfuls into the sauerkraut and water and cook for 8 to 10 minutes. Remove the roasting pan from the heat and put the pork pieces back in the pan with the sauerkraut for serving.

177

Old Christmas

Old Christmas fell on a Saturday this year, so it seemed like an extended weekend. In observance of this special day, we fasted from the evening of January 5 through the noon hour on January 6. All the adults in the church fast, unless they can't for health reasons.

So on Saturday morning, I made a light breakfast for the children. You aren't expected to fast until you are a church member (after adult baptism). After the children ate, we spent the morning reading the Bible, reading to the children, and reading psalms. Then, when the noon hour arrived we broke our fast with a meal. I fixed eggs, potatoes, bacon, toast, and cheese. Sometimes after fasting I will fry a chicken, but this time we had a "late breakfast" type meal.

After eating, we all washed the dishes, some of the children took a nap, and others read. It was a quiet day around here in observance of Old Christmas. Since it was Saturday, we had church services the next day, so the evening was spent giving the children baths and preparing our church clothes. The quiet of Old Christmas makes it feel like a Sunday.

Old Christmas wasn't observed as much in the Amish community in Berne, Indiana, where we lived before coming to Michigan. But here they do observe it. Seems some Amish communities celebrate it, while others don't. In Berne, the factories wouldn't consider it a "day off," because not many people observed it. Around here, the factories (run and owned by non-Amish) will actually shut down on Old Christmas because they have so many Amish employees.

VALENTINE'S DAY

As is the case with many secular observances, Amish participation in Valentine's Day varies greatly from place to place. Most, however, let February 14 pass without notice. Amish children who attend public school may make a handmade Valentine to bring home to Mom, but even that would be the exception rather than the rule. So, if you're Amish, don't expect chocolates, roses, or jewelry on this day!

BIRTHDAYS

With ten of us, our family's calendar is always full of birthdays. The first one to arrive each year is my daughter Susan's, on January 24. Most years, I let the children pick out whatever they want for supper on their special day. A typical birthday meal for one of my children is usually pizza, which seems to be a favorite for all of them. The pizza is usually accompanied by ice cream and cakes. We'll put the number of candles on the cake for the child's age, or sometimes we do cupcakes. One year, we put eleven candles on eleven cupcakes. If you include our sister Emma and her family that live nearby, plus my sisters Susan and Verena, that would be a lot of birthdays to try to get us all together for each one. So usually our children's birthdays are a celebration with just us, though the others come when they can. Of course, we sing "Happy Birthday," and we always try to get each child a gift. One year, Susan wanted a book about tornadoes. She is quick to get scared when it storms, so I think she finds reading about the weather interesting and comforting. Sometimes the more you know about something the less scary it is for you. Each of our children has his or her own unique personality.

CHOCOLATE SHEET CAKE

Serves 25 to 30

This is a really moist cake and very easy for children to make (and eat!). Our daughter Elizabeth usually makes this cake for us. One year, she made it for Joe to take to work on his birthday. This cake works well for us because of its large size, because when our family gets together with Jacob and Emma's family to celebrate a birthday, a 9 by 13-inch cake isn't big enough anymore!

2 cups all-purpose flour

2 cups sugar

1 teaspoon baking soda

1 teaspoon salt

½ cup (1 stick) margarine or butter

1 cup water

¼ cup unsweetened cocoa powder

2 large eggs, beaten

½ cup sour cream

½ cup milk

1 teaspoon vanilla extract

ICING

½ cup (1 stick) margarine or butter

6 teaspoons milk

¼ cup unsweetened cocoa powder

1 pound powdered sugar, sifted

1 teaspoon vanilla extract

½ cup chopped walnuts (optional)

Preheat the oven to 350°F. Grease a 10 by 15-inch baking pan.

Combine the flour, sugar, baking soda, and salt in a large bowl. Stir with a whisk to blend. Combine the margarine, water, and cocoa in a medium saucepan and bring to a boil over medium heat. Add the hot mixture to the dry ingredients and stir well. Add the eggs and beat well, then add the sour cream, milk, and vanilla.

Pour the batter into the pan and bake until a toothpick inserted in the center comes out clean, 20 to 25 minutes. Remove from the oven and let cool completely.

To make the icing: Combine the margarine, milk, and cocoa in a large saucepan. Gradually stir in the powdered sugar until smooth; stir in the vanilla until blended.

Spread the icing over the cooled cake and sprinkle with nuts.

Note: If you don't have sour cream, you can mix 1 tablespoon distilled white vinegar into ½ cup of milk to make soured milk. That is what I always do when I don't have sour cream on hand.

DAD'S BIRTHDAY, FEBRUARY 17

A Tribute to Benjamin Coblentz (1931–2000)

When I think of my father, I think of a quiet, respectful man. He had a good sense of humor and liked to tease everyone. I remember as a child going to sit with him in church services. He would always give me a peppermint candy to suck on. Sometimes I would sit with him just long enough to get my candy and then hurry back to my mom. After a while, he started waiting to give me the candy so I would stay sitting beside him longer.

I remember helping him milk cows, haul manure, and mow and rake hay. He'd let me drive the team and go unload the manure spreader. But he always warned us to be careful.

He'd also let us girls mow or rake hay with the team of horses out in the sixteen-acre hayfield, although he would always walk behind to make sure we were all right or the mower didn't clog up. Dad was always willing to go help Joe and me after we were married. After Joe and I married, we lived in a trailer house on their property so we could save to one day get a place of our own. While we lived there, Joe and Dad became almost like father and son. I treasure the memory of my departed father and still miss him dearly.

WINTER WORK AND PLAY

It is always a bit of a relief when the holidays are over. It just seems like it is a rushed time, so the cold, snowy winter days following the holidays give us time to get caught up on indoor work and to just enjoy some slower-paced time together. There is nothing like an evening spent inside when the wind is whipping up the snow outside. Of course, if we do have to go someplace, it is much easier to do so here in Michigan, where we are permitted to have covered buggies!

Winter Buggy Rides

When we lived in Indiana, the Amish there used open buggies. Here in Michigan, the buggies are enclosed, which makes for a much warmer ride during the winter months. I think it is

cozy when you are riding and it is cold outside and you don't feel the wind. In the open buggies, you would have to wear really thick mittens to hold the umbrella, which was our only shield against the winter winds. The wind would sometimes be so strong I couldn't hold the umbrella. And I definitely couldn't enjoy the scenery when I was stuck behind the umbrella like I can in an enclosed buggy.

In the closed buggies, you are warm and can take time to look out the window at the falling snow and quiet landscape. A lot of buggies around here have propane heaters in them to keep warm, but with us having a family of ten in the buggy we wouldn't have room. Also, though, ten people create a lot of heat, so we really don't need it. Another thing is we don't have to haul as much clothing around. There were lots more coats, scarves, and thicker gloves to worry about in the open buggies.

GROSZVATER
by Elizabeth Eicher, age thirteen

My grandfather was always friendly and quiet, although he loved to joke and tease people. My hair was always messy, so he would say, "Go find some bailer twines in the barn and I'll braid your hair for you." Then I would run away and shout, "No, you can't, I won't let you."

I remember when Grandfather was sitting in a rocking chair close to the stove. Kevin Williams was close to the stove warming his hands, but then he stood too close and burned some holes in his pants. Grandfather tilted his head back and really laughed about that.

He loved to read. I remember on winter nights he'd sit and read a book, newspaper, or magazine. You'd always see him reading when he had spare time, which wasn't too often. I was about six when Grandfather passed away. I don't think I really understood then what had happened because I got tired of standing in front of the coffin. I was very scared when they put the coffin in the ground and started putting dirt on top of it. I didn't know how he was going to get out when he was finished sleeping. When Grandma died I finally kind of understood.

I think my grandpa was one of the best grandpas anyone could have had.

Snowstorms

The worst snow I can ever remember was back in 1978, when a big blizzard hit Indiana. I was only six years old at the time, but the memory that sticks with me the most is of all the milk. The cows still had to be milked, but the roads were impassable so there was no milk truck to haul it away as was usually the case. So we had milk stored in every container we could possibly find. We had milk all over the place.

The milk all stayed good because it was so cold. Then when the milkman did come, days and days later, Dad and my brothers, Albert and Amos, had to use dolly carts to get the cans out to the road because he was worried he would get stuck in our driveway.

In more recent times, when my daughter Susan was born, we had high drifts and the roads were closed for maybe two days. It was snowing and snowing, and after the Amish midwife left it became worse. Everyone was off work and school for a couple of days after that. I was so glad the baby came in time for the midwife to be there. The drifts were higher than the windows.

> **Kevin's note:** Home birthing is still by far the most common method of delivery among the Amish. Six of Lovina's eight children were born at home. An Amish mother may go the hospital to deliver if there are medical reasons. There is no set rule within the Amish church about where the delivery must take place; it's up to local custom and the wishes of the mother. Some states in recent years have attempted to crack down on home birthing or at least have a more regulated system of registering midwives. The Amish, however, often rely on self-taught Amish or Mennonite midwives to assist with births.

School Closings

Without a radio or TV, finding out whether public school is open or closed because of snow was always tough when I was in school. For most of the years, our milkman would come early and we would ask him, or our dad's work driver, and find out that way. Sometimes we would just have to wait it out. One time, we missed the bus because the school had a three-hour delay. Usually, after a two-hour delay we would change out of our school clothes and assume we were off for the day, so the three-hour delay really caught us by surprise. None of us were ready. Communication seems to be better here in Michigan.

Here in Michigan, we can have phones in the outside buildings. The school tells parents not to call to find out about closings, but without TV or radio we sometimes have to. So far, they haven't said anything about us Amish calling since they know we don't have television. Some of the Amish schools go by the public schools; they'll close when the public schools close—which isn't very often around here.

Winter Play

Snow gives our children so much enjoyment during the otherwise cold, dreary winter months. It's amazing how the imaginations of children can allow them to find so many different ways to play. I wouldn't want my children to have television; it just seems they use their imaginations so much more with reading, playing outdoors, and with one another. After a big snow, the children love to make a snowman or go out and make snow angels. Recently, after a fluffy snow, my four-year-old son, Joseph, lay down on the driveway and made an angel and then stood up and looked at it. Joseph asked if I thought God saw him making an angel. I told him I was sure He did.

The children also like to take a sled on top of a nearby hill and go down. They were having fun running and jumping on their sled. They allow them to bring sleds to school, since they have a hill there.

For the adults, you hardly see sleighs around here, like we had in the Amish community in Indiana. The roads are hillier here and it's not as easy to pull a sleigh. Still, we miss the sleighs and might try to have one here someday. Joe wants to get himself a sleigh made with a canvas top.

ONE MORE MONTH OF COLD!

It shows on the calendar it is still winter. My husband came in to ask who started to make a snowman outside, but it turns out no one had. All we could figure out was that high winds blowing across the fields whirled the snow around, blowing some snow into three neatly formed balls in a row. We had never seen anything like it.
—Elizabeth Coblentz, February 1994

February can be just as bone chilling and snowy as any of the other winter months, but there is a feeling toward the end of the month that spring is just around the corner. (Yes, March can still be cold, but by the time that month arrives we know warmth is just weeks away!) For most of the month, though, there are just the usual winter chores and routines. We eat more apples and drink more hot chocolate in the winter. That just seems to be a favorite indoor snack. But all the snow and ice gives us one special treat that isn't available to us as easily during the summer: ice cream.

HOMEMADE ICE CREAM
Serves 10 to 12

Homemade ice cream is something we have more of in the winter; after all, there is plenty of snow outside to pack around the hand-cranked churn. We usually just like our ice cream simple, flavored with vanilla. But there are some people around here who like to add a box of instant pudding, chocolate or butterscotch, to their ice cream. But I always just like it plain. The children enjoy a cold drink of cider with their ice cream during these winter months.

We use a hand-cranked ice cream freezer, which takes rock salt. We use snow as our ice, adding it in layers with the rock salt as we crank the freezer. For best results, follow the instructions on your own ice cream freezer.

7 large eggs

10 cups milk

3½ cups sugar

2 tablespoons vanilla extract

1 teaspoon salt

Beat the eggs in a large bowl until smooth. Stir in the milk, sugar, vanilla, and salt. Pour into an ice cream freezer and freeze according to the manufacturer's instructions. Enjoy!

Winter Quilting

Quilting is something passed down through the generations and years. Mom taught all of us sisters how to quilt. I remember one winter after Leah had married and moved out but the rest of us were still at home, we would get up at 4 A.M. to begin quilting. A few would do the dishes while the others would sit down to quilt. I learned to quilt when I was thirteen or fourteen. I would like to make quilts for my children, too, once they are all in school. Mom made us full-size quilts, so I can't use them on our bed. I'd like to make a quilt for a queen-size bed. I loved it when we could sit there and quilt, especially in the wintertime. Us girls would sing and talk and quilt.

I would like to start teaching my oldest daughter, Elizabeth, how to sew this summer. It is not really that hard to learn how to run the treadle sewing machine. First, Mom would make us sew seams and just practice. Mom was really picky about not sewing crooked. She wanted us to use a ruler and make sure we folded every seam under just right. Although at the time it was hard, I am now glad she was so picky. I don't let my kids go near the sewing machine when it is out, but someday I'll be glad to teach the girls to sew.

There are some areas where the machine is an advantage. For instance, when you sew a button on by hand you cannot make it as tight as you can by machine. It will stay on a lot longer when you do it by machine.

Winter Chores

Another tough part of winter in this household is just keeping track of all the clothing needed to keep warm. Winter has me bringing all the boots, caps, scarves, thicker snow pants, and hats out of storage. With eight children, this is quite a collection of clothes!

I have to have almost two or three winter coats for everyone because it can take two or three days for heavier coats to dry on the clothesline in our basement. Some of the children even have four coats. The girls wear head scarves, so we have a lot of those also. And gloves are everywhere in the winter. I couldn't tell you how many pairs of gloves we have around here, not to mention gloves missing a mate. Benjamin is my worst glove loser. He will always come home from school with one glove. Black gloves for the boys and pink or purple for the girls helps tell some apart. But most are a dark color.

Joe and I also have several coats. Joe has a work coat, a Sunday coat, and a chore coat for the barn chores. That is a lot of coats just for him, too. I have three coats myself, one for Sunday, one for going into town, and another for chores around the house. Storing all of these coats is a chore. I have two cedar chests upstairs, which helps a bit to store unused coats.

I also do more mending in the winter. Without the outdoor chores, I have a little more time to do that. I do a lot more baking in the cold winter months, also, as the oven helps warm the house up a bit, especially in the mornings. When I bake something, I like to bake in the morning. But before I start baking anything, I go to the barn and let the horses out of their stalls and into the fields. I also have to feed the chickens, and if the weather is really cold, their water troughs are frozen, so I take a little mallet and break the ice and give them more water. Also, morning requires that the ash pans from the coal stoves be dumped. This also has to be done in the evening. When the weather warms up toward spring, the pan may just need to be dumped once a day.

HOME BUTCHERING

Home butchering is a long tradition in our family, and with most Amish. Mom and Dad, for instance, would always raise some hogs and a steer for our own meat. We would have two or three hogs that we would raise from piglets, feed them all summer, and then slaughter the following winter. Dad didn't like to have too many hogs because he just thought they were messy and smelly.

Butchering hogs or a steer is something we always do in the winter. The work isn't as hot, stifling, or unpleasant as it is during the summer, and it's just a good time of year to stock up on meat.

PORK

Most of the hogs we butcher are three to four hundred pounds. We try to raise a few little piglets each year. In years when we haven't raised any of our own, we buy meat from Amish farmers in the area. We want to know that it is grass-fed and hormone-free.

The messiest job for the women is cleaning out the intestines in order to grind and stuff the sausage. We used to scald the hogs in a hot tank before butchering, but now we just skin them. When you skin them you lose more lard, but I find I don't use lard as often these days for health reasons. Joe likes it that I have switched more to olive oil. I usually give my lard to someone who will make soap from it.

Sometimes, we cook down the lard to make some of the cracklings. When we were children we ate them right after they were cool enough to eat. I remember taking a bag in to one of my schoolteachers who liked them a lot. I don't like them as much as when I was a kid, I think it's because I now know that cracklings are just cooked-down lard.

Mom would always offer to stay out and watch the kettles while the men went in to eat. Someone had to keep things stirred. While waiting by the pot and stirring, Mom would take the lungs, cook them, and eat them. She didn't waste any part of the

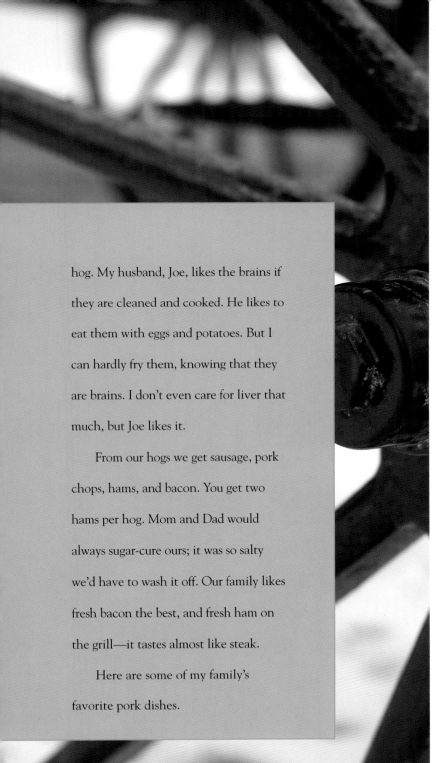

hog. My husband, Joe, likes the brains if they are cleaned and cooked. He likes to eat them with eggs and potatoes. But I can hardly fry them, knowing that they are brains. I don't even care for liver that much, but Joe likes it.

From our hogs we get sausage, pork chops, hams, and bacon. You get two hams per hog. Mom and Dad would always sugar-cure ours; it was so salty we'd have to wash it off. Our family likes fresh bacon the best, and fresh ham on the grill—it tastes almost like steak.

Here are some of my family's favorite pork dishes.

SWISS HAM BAKE
Serves 6 to 8

If the hog is big, you get two bigger hams per hog. Mom and Dad always sugar cured ours and used the meat in hearty recipes like this one. This is a layered casserole that definitely goes a long way in feeding a family of 10 or any company that might drop by.

8 tablespoons (1 stick) butter
½ cup chopped onion
½ cup chopped green bell pepper
1 (10¾-ounce) can condensed cream of mushroom soup
1 cup sour cream
8 ounces noodles, cooked and drained
2 cups shredded Swiss cheese
3 cups cubed cooked ham
1 cup fresh bread crumbs

Preheat the oven to 350°F. Butter a 3-quart casserole.

Melt 4 tablespoons of the butter in a medium skillet over medium heat and sauté the onion and bell pepper until soft, about 5 minutes. Stir in the soup and sour cream.

In the prepared dish, layer one-third of the noodles, one-third of the cheese, one-third of the ham, and half of the soup mixture. Make a second layer the same way. Make a third layer of ham, noodles, and cheese only.

Melt the remaining 4 tablespoons butter in a medium skillet and toss the bread crumbs to coat. Sprinkle the buttered crumbs evenly over the casserole. Bake until the casserole is bubbling and the cheese is melted, about 40 minutes.

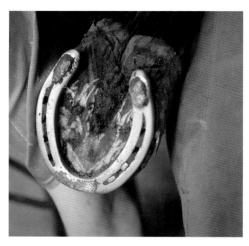  

SAUSAGE GRAVY

Makes about 4 quarts

When I fix this recipe, I usually fix about a gallon pot, which requires two or three pounds of sausage. Leftover portions can be refrigerated, but I don't think it's as good the second time around. I like to use my fresh sausage, but home-canned or store-bought can be used. Fresh sausage, I think, has a better flavor. We like to eat sausage gravy on biscuits.

1 pound bulk sausage

3 tablespoons all-purpose flour

8 cups whole milk, plus more as needed

Pinch of salt

Pinch of ground pepper

Crumble the sausage in a large skillet over medium heat and brown for 10 to 15 minutes. Add the flour to the sausage. Stir until the flour is blended in. Gradually stir in the milk. Let simmer for 3 to 5 minutes, stirring regularly. Add the salt and pepper. Taste and adjust the seasoning. Add more milk as needed, to the thickness you want it to be.

FARMER'S BREAKFAST
Serves 4 to 6

This turns out more like an omelette. We often like to enjoy "breakfast" for supper, since mornings are often so rushed around here. There is no better way to enjoy fresh pork than with eggs. This is a favorite way to serve fresh ham!

6 large eggs

2 tablespoons milk

Dash of salt

¼ teaspoon ground pepper

1 cup diced cooked ham

⅓ cup margarine or butter

2 potatoes, peeled and finely chopped

¼ cup sliced green onion, including green tops

Combine the eggs, milk, salt, and pepper in a large bowl and beat until smooth. Stir in the ham and set aside.

Melt the margarine or butter in a large skillet over medium heat and sauté the potatoes and onion, stirring frequently, until tender, 8 to 10 minutes. Pour the egg mixture over the potato mixture in the skillet. Cook without stirring until the mixture begins to set around the bottom and edges, about 3 or 4 minutes. Push back the edges to let the liquid run under and cook if you want to make an omelette, then fold it when cooked through, or just scramble the eggs.

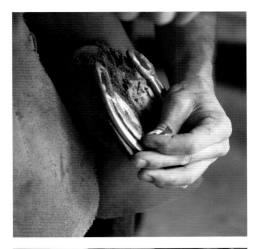

SAUSAGE AND NOODLE DINNER

Serves 8

You can use store-bought sausage for this recipe, but we always use fresh sausage. Although we do our butchering in the winter, recipes like this are enjoyed year-round, as I home-can some and freeze some.

1 pound bulk pork sausage

1 head cabbage (about 1½ pounds), cored and thinly sliced

1 large onion, thinly sliced

1 large carrot, peeled and shredded

2 teaspoons chicken soup base

¼ cup boiling water

2 cups sour cream

¾ teaspoon salt

½ teaspoon ground pepper

8 ounces noodles, freshly cooked and drained

Minced fresh parsley for garnish

Brown the sausage in a large skillet over medium heat. Drain the grease. Leave the sausage in the skillet and add the cabbage, onion, and carrot and mix well. Dissolve the chicken soup base in the boiling water and add to the pot. Cover and cook over medium heat until the vegetables are tender, 10 to 15 minutes.

Reduce the heat under the skillet to low and stir in the sour cream, salt, and pepper. Transfer the mixture to a large serving bowl, add the hot noodles, and toss. Garnish with parsley.

BEEF

I'd rather butcher a steer than a hog. A steer has fewer steps. You can get a lot of meat from a steer. If it is a pretty big steer, then the meat we get from it can feed our whole family for a year or more! The steer is definitely less greasy than the hog. With the beef, all you do is cut off all the meat. Wherever we see there are nice steaks, we make sure to get them first. Then we cut up the leaner meat pieces for "beef chunks" to be used in stews and soups. The meat that has a bit more fat I save to grind up.

Most of the time, we will butcher a steer that is 1,400 to 1,800 pounds. One year, we butchered an 1,100 pound steer, and that was a small one. We feed our steer grass and then maybe hay in the wintertime.

It is good to freeze the meat before butchering, so during winter you can hang it in an outdoor shed for a couple of days before butchering. Some years it has been so cold that we've had to put the meat on tables inside overnight to let it start to thaw before the next morning. Our hands get so cold working on the near-frozen meat.

One year on steer-butchering day, Emma and Jacob came and stayed overnight so we could get right at it in the morning. Verena, Susan, Emma, and Jacob all spent the day here cutting up the quarters of beef as soon as the children left for school. We had two folding tables in the basement. The tables held four quarters of beef. Overall it was 1,100 pounds of meat. The beef bones were cooked off and used to make vegetable soup (see Grandma's Soup, page 99). Mom would always cook a bone, add cabbage leaves, and make a really good broth. She also added a few vegetables.

My favorite part of the steer is a good piece of steak, which we slice really thin and put in a skillet. We add enough oil or grease to come 2 inches up the side of the pan, or more if we're deep frying. We heat the pan on high heat and put the meat in just long enough to brown it on both sides, and that is it. We call the dish "rare beef." This is something my family has enjoyed for generations.

My grandpa would pepper it heavily on each side, and I think that is something my mother picked up because she would also. Joe doesn't think I put enough pepper on, so he is always there with the pepper shaker putting more on.

Most of the rest of the meat gets either canned in jars and processed, or packed for the freezer. For canning, every quart needs to be processed for 90 minutes, and with only seven-quart jars able to fit into a pressure cooker, meat canning can be a couple of days' work. I have two pressure cookers, and sometimes I borrow one from my sisters to speed things up.

Here are some of our family's favorite beef recipes.

POOR MAN'S STEAK

Serves 6 to 8

This is an easy, delicious dish that is served a lot at weddings, young peoples' gatherings, and Sunday-evening suppers when we might have people who attended church in the morning at our place back over for a meal. Poor Man's Steak looks a bit like slices of fried steak with gravy poured over. Note that it needs to be started in the morning of the day you will eat it for supper.

1 pound ground beef

1 cup milk

¼ teaspoon ground pepper

1 cup crushed saltine crackers

1 teaspoon salt

1 small onion, finely chopped

1 (10¾-ounce) can condensed cream of mushroom soup

Combine the ground beef, milk, pepper, cracker crumbs, salt, and onion in a large bowl and stir to blend. Shape the mixture into a narrow loaf with your hands and put it on a plate. Let it sit in the refrigerator, covered, for at least 8 hours or overnight.

Preheat the oven to 325°F. Remove the loaf from the oven, cut it into ¾-inch-thick slices, and fry in a large skillet until browned, about 2 minutes on each side. Put the fried slices in layers in a large roasting pan and spread cream of mushroom soup over all. Bake until the mixture is nice and bubbly, about 1 hour.

FRESH GROUND BEEF SUPPER

Serves 6 to 8

With a family of ten, large help-yourself casseroles like this are good. This will feed a big family easily!

1 pound ground beef

½ cup chopped onion

1 cup chopped green bell pepper

1 pound tomatoes, diced

½ cup white long-grain rice

2 teaspoons chili powder

½ teaspoon salt

⅛ teaspoon ground pepper

2 cups shredded mozzarella cheese

Preheat the oven to 350°F.

In a large skillet, brown the beef over medium-high heat. Drain the grease. Add the onion and bell pepper. Stir in the tomatoes, rice, chili powder, salt, and pepper and heat thoroughly.

Pour the mixture into an ungreased 8-cup casserole dish. Cover and bake for 50 minutes. Sprinkle the cheese evenly on top and bake, uncovered, for about 10 minutes more, or until the cheese is melted and the casserole is bubbling.

DELICIOUS BAKED MEATBALLS

Serves 6

Fresh ground beef makes for the best meatballs! After using beef from your own steer, eating other meatballs isn't as enjoyable. We like to add a dash of chili powder to add some spice to them.

MEATBALLS

1 cup milk

3 pounds ground beef

2 cups old-fashioned rolled oats

2 large eggs, beaten

1 cup chopped onion

½ teaspoon garlic powder

2 teaspoons salt

½ teaspoon ground pepper

2 teaspoons chili powder

SAUCE

2 cups ketchup

1½ cups packed brown sugar

½ teaspoon garlic powder

½ cup chopped onion

2 tablespoons liquid hickory smoke (optional)

Preheat the oven to 350°F.

Combine the milk, ground beef, oats, and eggs in a large bowl and mix with your hands until well blended. Stir in the onion, garlic powder, and seasonings. Shape the mixture into 1½- to 2-inch balls and put them in a roasting pan. Set aside.

To make the sauce: Stir all the sauce ingredients together in a medium bowl. Pour over the meatballs. Bake until meatballs are browned and cooked through, about 50 minutes.

BEEF CASSEROLE

Serves 6 to 8

This is a hearty, beefy casserole to enjoy. What makes it different are the biscuits on top. The biscuits sort of sink down into the casserole and end up almost covering the top. Don't bake the biscuits, just put them on top of this casserole.

1 package of refrigerated biscuits

1½ pounds ground beef

½ cup chopped onion

1 (8-ounce) package cream cheese, softened

1 (10¾-ounce) can cream of chicken or mushroom soup

¼ cup milk

1 teaspoon salt

¼ cup ketchup

Preheat the oven to 375°F. Grease an 8-cup casserole dish.

Brown the beef with the onion in a large skillet over medium heat, about 10 minutes. Drain the grease.

Combine the cream cheese, soup, milk, salt, and ketchup in a medium bowl. Stir to blend. Add to the ground beef and stir well. Spoon into the prepared dish.

Bake for 10 minutes. Place the unbaked biscuits on top. Return the casserole to the oven and bake until the biscuits are browned and cooked through, 10 to 15 minutes.

AMISH SNOWBIRDS

While frigid temperatures and cold, blustery sheets of wind-driven snow whiten the American Midwest, the Amish hunker down in their homes, warmed by coal and kerosene stoves. These harsh winters can take their toll on the elderly and grow tiresome for some. So some sun-seeking Amish choose, at least for a few weeks, to escape. The Amish answer to the winter blahs: Pinecraft, Florida.

You won't find Pinecraft featured in any glossy travel brochures, but for winter-weary Amish, this is their answer to Walt Disney World. Pinecraft is the name of a small Amish enclave tucked away in a corner of bustling Sarasota, Florida. It's the only Amish community in the state, and it attracts Pennsylvania Dutch—Amish and Mennonite—snowbirds from all over the United States. Pinecraft provides a restful place with a curative climate, especially for elderly Amish wishing to escape brutal Midwestern winters.

My first visit to Pinecraft was in November 2004. November is the beginning of Pinecraft's busy season, when the Amish-Mennonite population swells to over five thousand by mid- to late January. A "skeletal" community of Amish do live here year-round, but for the most part it's a transient population of comers and goers who inhabit thimble-sized cottages for weeks at a time before heading back home.

Life in Pinecraft is a relaxing retreat from days filled with chores and strict rules. A few Amish-style restaurants serve up hearty Pennsylvania Dutch fare, adding a slightly touristy feel to the area. The post office and the Mennonite Traveler's Church serve as the hub of the community, where news is learned and gossip exchanged. An Amish-Mennonite parochial school operates in the winter to provide school instruction to youngsters traveling with their families. Most of the rifts and rivalries that divide Amish communities "up north" disappear in the laid-back sunshine of Florida. Buggies are nowhere to be found; instead they are replaced with adult tricycles. Pinecraft is a compact enough area that walking or cycling is the most practical means of transport. Besides, Sarasota city ordinances don't permit horse-drawn buggies on the roads. Amish families, in their traditional plain clothing, can be seen frequenting the nearby beach and sampling the sun.

The community's roots here began in the 1920s, when Amish farmers were lured south with promises of fertile farmland for raising celery crops. The promises turned out to be false, but some Amish decided to stay. Some of the visiting Amish arrive by train or private hired vans. Others take the chartered bus affectionately named the "Snowbird Express." The bus runs weekly during the height of winter.

Sometimes snow holds on late here in Michigan.
I remember one year when the snows fell well into April.
But no matter how long winter tries to hang on, spring
always wins in the end. The tulips will be bright,
the birds will scout out my hanging pots for nesting space,
and the wild rhubarb will unfurl its large leaves.
And we'll begin another year.

Index